GARLAND STUDIES IN

ENTREPRENEURSHIP

edited by

STUART BRUCHEY
UNIVERSITY OF MAINE

A GARLAND SERIES

THE RISE OF HOTEL CHAINS IN THE UNITED STATES 1896–1980

PAUL L. INGRAM

GARLAND PUBLISHING, INC.
NEW YORK & LONDON / 1996

Library of Congress Cataloging-in-Publication Data

Ingram, Paul L., 1967–
The rise of hotel chains in the United States, 1896–1980 / Paul L. Ingram.
p. cm. — (Garland studies in entrepreneurship)
Includes bibliographical references and index.
ISBN 0-8153-2649-1 (alk. paper)
1. Hotel chains—United States—History—20th century. 2. Hotel chains—United States—History—19th century. I. Title. II. Series.
TX910.U5I53 1996
338.7'61647947301—dc20 96-25078

Printed on acid-free, 250-year-life paper
Manufactured in the United States of America

To My Parents

CONTENTS

FIGURES

TABLES

PREFACE

The purpose of this book is to provide a rigorous, theoretically informed account of the rise of hotel chains. I see three contributions from this effort. First, the specific industry and phenomenon that is studied is interesting and important to the American economy. The hotel industry is a big one, and chains are now the dominant form of organization in that industry. Second, the rise of chains in general is a critical and understudied event in recent economic history. Chains dominate, or are coming to dominate, all service industries. Service industries are becoming increasingly important in the American and world economy. Those facts combine to suggest that chains deserve the close attention of researchers of organizations, yet there is surprisingly little systematic research on chains. This book represents the first stage of my continuing effort to understand the chain form of organization. Third, the evolution of organizational forms in the hotel industry may be informative on the relationship between organizations and their environments. I follow recent practice in organizational theory by examining the effect of the environment on organizations, but I also use historical analysis to identify the role of organizations and entrepreneurs in affecting the environment.

To explain the rise of chains, I combine history, theory, and statistical analyses. The first five chapters consider the history of the hotel industry in the United States and findings from organizational theory to derive predictions for the evolution of hotel chains. The second half of the book, from the sixth chapter on, reports results of statistical analyses using a data set I have collected that represents every hotel chain that existed in the United States between 1896 and 1980. These data allow me to conduct dynamic statistical analyses of founding, failure, and growth of hotel chains. The statistical results support the predictions for the rise of hotel chains developed from history and theory. The combination of these methods gives me much more confidence than if I had merely considered the history of the industry, or performed statistical analyses without considering the action and perceptions of the entrepreneurs who make up the industry.

Much of the research reported in this book was conducted while I was a doctoral candidate at Cornell University where I began the task of collecting data on hotel chains in the Fall of 1992. I have continued to study hotel chains and the hotel industry since leaving Cornell, and I am currently involved in a number of projects that are extensions of the research presented in this book. I have tried to maintain the focus of the book on the basic influences on the rise of hotel chains, but where appropriate I have referenced other work, some of which examines in greater detail arguments presented here.

Like most people who conduct a research project of the scale of the one reported here, I received emotional support and encouragement from my family. Their contribution to this project also included a more concrete component. They were my research assistants and without them the timely completion of this book would have been impossible. My parents Bridget and Colin spent days accurately coding thousands of pages of hotel chain directories. My brother Patrick worked conscientiously to input the data into a computer. They brought the type of enthusiasm and dedication to the task that money can't buy (at least not cheaply!).

Tal Simons provided lavish amounts of encouragement and friendship. Tal also critiqued, discussed, and proof-read much of this work. The inspiration to study hotel chains came from discussions on the squash court with Crist Inman. Crist was also a great help in collecting data and was always willing to debate our mutual interest in institutional change. Colin Ingram and Colin Osburn each read and critiqued complete drafts of this book, providing many useful comments.

John Freeman gave me inside information about doing research on organizations that would have otherwise taken a whole career to acquire. John's confidence in me was a great source of motivation. Bob Gibbons often pushed me to clarify my arguments and some of the most interesting ideas in this book began in his Economics of Organization seminar. Victor Nee introduced me to ideas that are at the core of this book and will continue to affect my work. Even more importantly he imparted to me an excitement for social science. Phil Anderson was always willing to give me practical advice, even after he had left Cornell.

Many people helped me to find the data used here. In particular I'd like to acknowledge Susan Schwartz, the staff of Cornell's hotel library, and the staff of the American Hotel and Motel Association archives in Washington.

I gratefully acknowledge the generous support of the Social Sciences and Humanities Research Council of Canada. That organization provided me with a Doctoral Fellowship for three years during which much of this book was completed. The Faculty Development Fund of Carnegie Mellon University also gave me a grant that was helpful as I completed this book.

Paul Ingram

The Rise of Hotel Chains in the United States 1896–1980

1

The Rise of Organizational Forms

This book describes a transformation in the form of organization in the hospitality industry. Traditionally, that industry consisted of owner-operated organizations. During the twentieth century hotel chains, which are professionally managed, multi-unit organizations, have risen to prominence. The rise of hotel chains is a significant development for participants and customers of the hospitality industry, and for students of organizations and the American economy. The decline in importance of independent hotels represented an end to a way of life for small town hoteliers. The rise of hotel chains caused new patterns of competition among hospitality organizations and created new opportunities for employees in the hospitality industry by necessitating a range of managerial roles that did not exist for independent hotels. Chains also allow customers to interact with the same organization when traveling across the country, which reduces their uncertainty, and improves the expectation of good service from patronizing a hotel. More generally, the transformation to professionally managed organizations from owner-operated organizations is itself important because it has happened or is threatening to happen in so many industries.

The transformation in organizational form is partly demonstrated by the growth in the number of hotel chains, shown in Figure 1–1. In 1896 there were three hotel chains in the United States, managing about thirteen hotels. By 1980 there were more than 300 chains managing more than 10,000 hotels. The hotel chain form has grown much faster than the industry. A small fraction of one percent of hotel rooms were part of chains in 1900, 15% were by 1930, and by 1980 more than 50% of hotel rooms were managed by chains. Associated with the growth in chains and rooms managed by chains is consistent growth in the share of hospitality industry revenue earned by chains, shown in Figure 1–2. In 1987 hotel chains accounted for $28 billion of revenue.

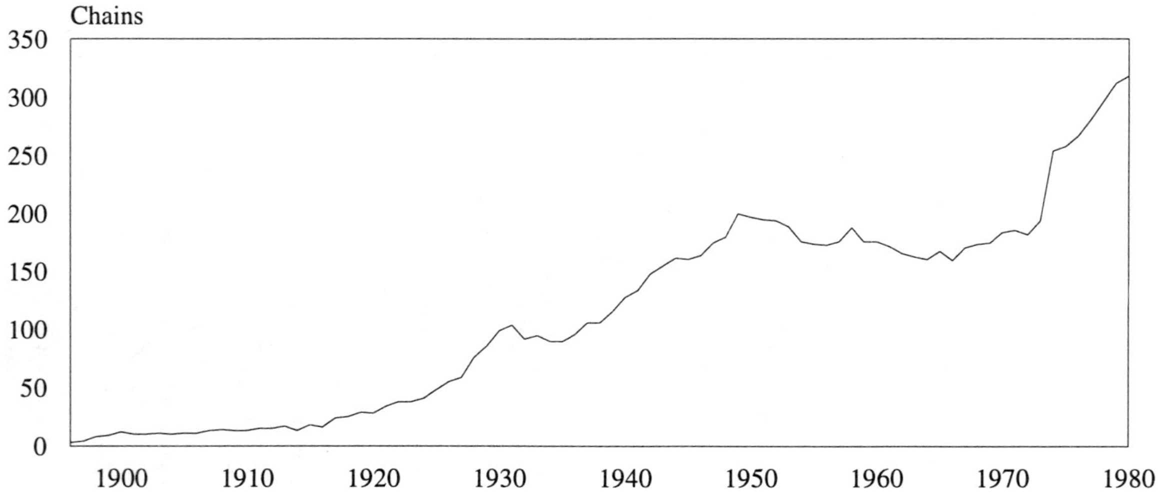

Figure 1-1. Number of Hotel Chains.

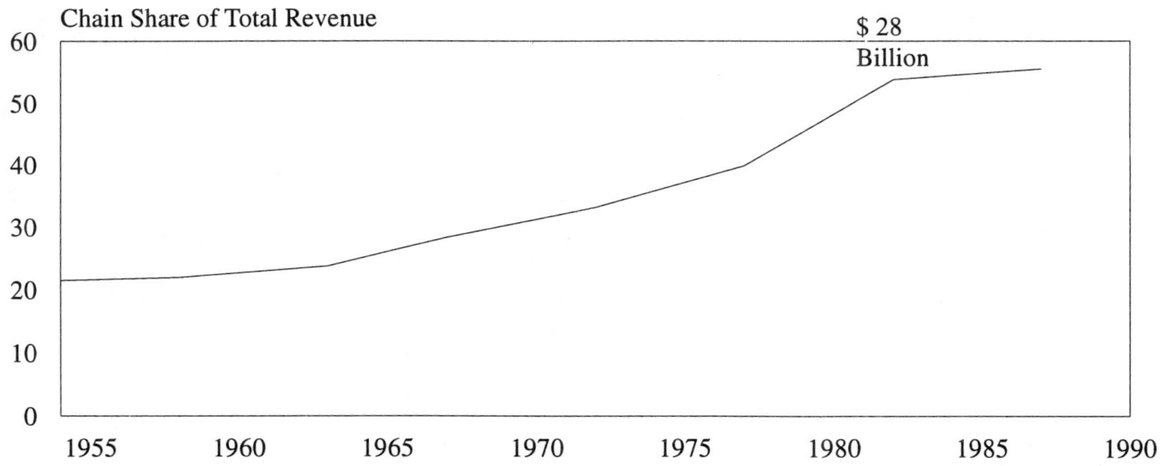

Figure 1-2. Percentage of Total Hotel Revenue Earned by Chains.
Source: U.S. Census of Business

The transformation to hotel chains also provides an opportunity to examine ideas about why one form of organization rather than another is used in an industry. Most of organizational theory in the last twenty years has been about the determinants of success for organizational forms. The influential arguments on this problem conclude that the environment organizations face, which consists of other organizations, technology, customers, laws and social norms, determines which form of organization will be successful. My position in this book builds on the idea that environments are fundamental determinants of organizational form, but differs from recent organizational theory by explicitly considering the role of entrepreneurs and organizations in influencing the environment. Some elements of the environment, for example government regulation, can be influenced by organizations and other interested actors. Consistent with the implications of this argument, I examine not only the influence of the environment on hotel chains, but the role of hotel-chain entrepreneurs and others in affecting the elements of the environment that matter for hotel chains. The elements of the environment that I focus on are the institutions that define the form of training in the hospitality industry, and the technology that allows owners of hotels to control their employees.

The rest of this chapter is dedicated to outlining the dominant theoretical explanations for the rise of organizational forms. I will concentrate on three streams of organizational theory: transaction cost economics, institutional theory and organizational ecology. The purpose of reviewing these theories is to generate an understanding of the possible influences on the rise of hotel chains as provided by research in other contexts, and to provide background for the theoretical contribution of this book. The chapters that follow develop the explanation of the rise of hotel chains. The second half of this book supports the arguments in the first half with detailed statistical analyses of the evolution of hotel chains in the United States.

TRANSACTION COST ECONOMICS AND EFFICIENCY ARGUMENTS

Transaction cost economics explains the prevalence of organizational forms with efficiency arguments. The short explanation for the existence of large professionally managed organizations is "because they are more efficient in some circumstances." The seeds of this approach were planted by Coase (1937) where the idea of using the transaction as the unit of analysis is introduced. In this classic work, questions such as why do firms exist at all and how large should firms be expected to be are addressed. Coase's answers are essentially the same as the ones that economists such as Oliver Williamson and Alfred Chandler offer fifty years later. Williamson and Chandler represent the core of the transaction cost position as it is currently expressed.

Williamson has made his arguments in a number of articles and books, most notably *Markets and Hierarchies* (1975). A key departure from neo-classical economics is the use of the transaction as the unit of analysis and the resulting focus on transaction costs. Williamson has a broad classification for transaction costs, which includes all costs not associated with production. The most basic question he addresses is which economic transactions should be governed by markets and which should be governed by hierarchies (organizations). The answer is that it depends on the nature of the transaction. The three critical dimensions of the transaction are: the degree of uncertainty involved in fully completing the transaction, the size of transaction-specific investments, and the frequency of recurrence of the transaction (Williamson 1979). Generally, the higher the uncertainty, idiosyncratic investment, and frequency of a transaction, the more appropriate it is to be governed within an organization.

Williamson recognizes that his approach can also be used to explain more subtle variations in organization than simply markets versus hierarchies. He summarizes his position on organizational design as:

> consistent with the general thrust of the Markets and Hierarchies approach, organization design is addressed as a transaction cost issue, and economizing purposes are emphasized. The general argument is this: except when there are perversities associated with the funding process, or when strategically situated members of an organization are unable to participate in the prospective gains, unrealized efficiency opportunities always offer an incentive to reorganize. (Williamson and Ouchi 1981a, 355)

So, the form of organization in an industry can be expected to be the most efficient form in transaction cost and scale economy terms.

The problem Chandler examines in *The Visible Hand* (1977) is a special case of the efficiency argument, and directly relevant to this study. By considering the rise of managerial capitalism in industrial enterprises in the late nineteenth century, Chandler examines the industrial counterpart to the transition in service industries that is the subject of the empirical component of this book. He argues that new technology created large increases in the economies of scale available to manufacturers. Therefore, producers found themselves in a position to supply much larger markets than they had previously. This presented a number of problems of coordination throughout the distribution chain which were solved by vertical integration, creating huge, professionally managed organizations that dominated their industries. The role of the manager changed to meet the opportunities presented by these changes.

Like Williamson, Chandler's justification for the prominence of an organizational form is its efficiency advantages. Chandler identifies the advantages of the vertically integrated, professionally managed organization as those of coordination (which Williamson and Ouchi [1981b] claim as a type of transaction cost). By embedding the general argument in a historical transformation, Chandler is successful at illustrating that the advantage of an organizational form depends on the circumstances: "the visible hand of the managers took over when unit costs were lowered through administrative coordination, and this situation occurred in manufacturing when the technology of production permitted the volume output of standardized products to national and international markets" (Chandler 1981).

Perhaps the most frequently offered criticism of the efficiency argument concerns the variation that remains on the organizational landscape. Perrow (1981) wonders why, if there are such advantages to vertical integration, GM and Ford still contract out for so much of their material requirements, and Boeing does not own an Airline. Similarly, Hamilton and Biggart (1988) observe that Japan, South Korea and Taiwan each have internal transportation and communication systems analogous to the ones that Chandler related to the growth of managerial capitalism in the United States. However, economic organization in these countries varies, and is dissimilar from that found in the U.S.

Despite its popularity with sociologists, this criticism amounts to little more than a caricature of the efficiency perspective. It ignores the basic contingency nature of transaction cost explanations. The form of governance that is most efficient for a type of transaction depends on the case, and although certain factors such as transportation technology dictate efficiency in one circumstance, they may not in another. As Daems has noted (1983, 42), "the superiority of a particular institutional arrangement is not absolute but is dependent on the *specific* needs for information and compliance (Daem's emphasis)." So, Boeing does not vertically integrate because the nature of its transactions makes vertical integration less efficient. Japan, South Korea and Taiwan differ in economic organization because they differ on characteristics other than transportation and communication technologies.

The same features that allow the efficiency position to respond to the above challenge lead to a more substantial criticism. Granovetter (1985) has accused Williamson of relying on bad functional explanations. The problem efficiency theorists have is that they don't explain how efficient forms are created and come to dominate. Williamson hints that an implicit Darwinian process is at work when he makes statements such as "over time those integration moves that have better rationality properties (in transaction cost and scale-economy terms) tend to have better survival properties" (Williamson and Ouchi 1981b, 389). However, the mere implication of a Darwinian selection process is not a sufficient response to the charge of bad functionalism. To support the expectation that efficient organizational forms will dominate it is necessary that (1) powerful selection pressures toward efficiency be operating and (2) there is some source of variation that creates the efficient organizational forms in the first place. There are challenges to both of these conditions. Despite this, "the operation of alleged selection pressures is [to Williamson] neither an object of study nor even a falsifiable proposition but rather an article of faith" (Granovetter 1985, 503).

It might be expected that Chandler's focus on historical dynamics would allow him to avoid the trap of bad functionalism, but it does not. This is particularly obvious in his explanation of the development of management. In that explanation, managers appear to change effortlessly to meet the needs of modern business enterprises. Large integrated firms require specialized skills so managers become increasingly technical and professional (Chandler's 1977 proposition 5). Brief recognition is made of the creation of business schools, professional associations and journals for managers, but nothing is said about the motives of the actors responsible. The impression given is that these things simply came into being as part of a society-wide recognition of the efficiency advantages of the professionally managed enterprise.

The criticism of efficiency arguments as bad functionalism suggests that their failing is in fact the opposite of what Hamilton and Biggart (1988, S67) suggest when they accuse Williamson and Chandler of concentrating their whole causal argument on proximate factors. It is not that efficiency theorists "argue that the assassination of Archduke Ferdinand caused World War I" but rather that they offer a plausible underlying cause for observed forms of organization (efficiency) but fail to explain how those forms came to exist and dominate. And without an explanation of the creation and growth of efficient forms, the argument that things are the way they are because of efficiency rings hollow.

INSTITUTIONAL THEORY

A problem with reviewing institutional explanations for the development of organizational forms is that there are a number of institutional theories (Scott 1987a). Beyond the distinct versions, the theory has recently had a "creeping" quality, expanding in response to challenges to the point that now there are probably no organizational or economic phenomena that are not claimed by someone to be institutional. So, in order to consider institutional explanations for the development of organizational forms it is necessary to be strict. I will break institutional theory into what I feel are its two main expressions, the first treating institutions as rationalized, taken-for-granted elements of society and the second treating institutions as systems of social rules that define networks of social organization and exchange. I will refer to these versions as the preconscious and the conscious positions, reflecting their claims about the mechanisms by which institutions constrain actors. The preconscious position is best represented by Meyer and Rowan's (1977) classic article. They argue that institutional rules (defined as "classifications built into society as reciprocated typifications or interpretations," p.341):

> have effects on organizational structures and their implementation in actual technical work which are very different from the effects generated by the networks of social behavior and relationships which compose and surround a given organization. (341)

In other words, institutions matter for themselves, and are not simply another dimension of exchange relationships. Actors comply with institutional rules to get legitimacy. Often legitimacy is accompanied by more material rewards such as positive evaluation by actors who supply the organization with resources, but these rewards do not explain institutional compliance. Organizations may adopt institutionalized myths to increase legitimacy "independent of the immediate efficacy of the acquired practices and procedures" (Meyer and Rowan 1977, 340). In fact, institutional forces may have such a strong taken-for-granted character as to be invisible to the actors they influence (DiMaggio 1988). As Oliver (1991, 148) notes, "institutional theory illustrates how the exercise of strategic choice may be pre-empted when organizations are unconscious of, blind to, or otherwise take for granted the institutional processes to which they adhere. Moreover, when external norms or practices obtain the status of a social fact, organizations may engage in activities that are not so much calculative and self-interested as obvious or proper."

Efforts of the preconscious position to explain organizational forms focus on diffusion processes. The basic argument begins with an organizational form being adopted, perhaps for efficiency reasons, by some organizations. As more organizations adopt the form (Tolbert and Zucker 1983) and as powerful institutional actors champion the form (Strang 1987) its legitimacy increases which encourages further diffusion. Tolbert and Zucker (1983) applied this argument to explain civil service reform. Their empirical findings were that early adoptions of civil service reform could be predicted by city characteristics that made reform rational, while later adoptions could not. Tolbert (1985) found that colleges had administrative structures reflective of their control. Public colleges had officers to administer relations to the public sector independent of actual funding from the public sector, while private colleges had officers to administer relations to the private sector independent of actual funding from the private sector. Strang (1987) argued that central actors prefer to interact with large bureaucracies and found that school district consolidation increased as a function of state funding.

These empirical studies all illustrate a problem the preconscious position has with explaining the rise of professionally managed organizations like hotel chains. None of these three studies, and very few studies in this tradition (Haveman 1993a and Hamilton and Biggart 1988) explain the organizational forms of for-profit enterprises. In fact, the theory itself claims that environments differ in the relative importance of their institutional and technical features (Meyer and Rowan 1977), and institutional influences are more important to organizations in the public sphere (Meyer and Scott 1983).

Another common feature in empirical work supporting the preconscious position is a "black-box" characteristic. Legitimacy, the factor that explains conformity to institutional pressures, is never operationalized. Instead, what is demonstrated is a relationship between the rise of an institution and the rise of an organizational form, or the difficulty of using rationality arguments to explain the rise of an organizational form. This indirect strategy of support invites alternative explanations. A particularly compelling alternative concerns the economics of information. Herd theory (for instance, Scharfstein and Stein 1990) suggests that when managers have imperfect information (which is almost always) there are circumstances when their best action is to conform to what they see other managers doing, or "follow the herd." When some managers have information and others don't, the managers with information will be most likely to act and managers without information can make up for their deficiency by following the informed managers. When some managers have good information and others have bad information, the good information will be strongly correlated while the bad information will be drawn from a wide range of possible delusions, so organizations doing the same thing are probably those organizations whose managers have good information. This theory predicts conformity among organizations because of strictly rational reasons: if you are uncertain, see what others are doing. Further, herd theory and institutional theory also predict that the same types of organizations will lead diffusion waves. Central organizations, organizations who are large and successful and organizations that have access to governments and other regulatory agents are likely to be the ones with the best information and therefore the best to follow.

Finally, the most damning criticism of the preconscious form of institutional theory is its failure to explain the origin and change of institutions (Brint and Karabel 1990). The growth of an organizational form is a dynamic process. Therefore, the argument that organizational forms result from institutional influence is not satisfactory unless an explanation for changes in institutional influence is also offered. The phenomenon being studied is a change in organization, so it cannot be explained by unchanging institutional forces. The inability of the preconscious position to explain institutional creation and change may result directly from its preconscious mechanism of institutional influence. Since actors are unaware of the institutions that constrain them they cannot intentionally influence those institutions. Unable to appeal to individual or group motives, the preconscious position flounders in what DiMaggio (1988) has called a metaphysical pathos.

It is largely in response to that metaphysical pathos that the second, conscious institutionalism developed. As DiMaggio (1988, 11) observed:

> without more explicit attention to interest and agency of the kind that institutional rhetoric has thus far obstructed, institutional theorists will be unable to develop predictive and persuasive accounts of the origins, reproduction, and erosion of institutionalized practices and organizational forms.

Since attention to interest and agency is precluded by a theory that claims institutions preempt strategic action, the obvious necessity is to reconsider the mechanism of institutional influence. What if actors, rather than simply taking institutions for granted, were conscious of them and responded to them based on consideration of the associated rewards and punishments?

This opens up a wide range of possible strategic responses to institutional pressure. Actors that can fit institutional constraints into the rational calculus that determines their conscious action may decide to acquiesce, compromise, defy or even manipulate institutional pressure (Oliver 1991).

When institutions are seen as conscious constraints on action, attention turns to the rewards and punishments that accompany them. In DiMaggio and Powell's (1983) first two hypotheses concerning institutional isomorphism, they identify resource dependence as a predictor of the institutional influence of one organization over another. Consistent with the resource dependence characterization, Nee and Ingram (1997) have suggested that exchange theory can be used to analyze institutional influence. In this view, institutions are social rules governing exchange. Since the conscious view of institutions is consistent with exchange theory, it is not surprising that there is an economic theory parallel to the sociological one. Douglass North (North 1990; Davis and North 1971) suggests that institutions form a framework of incentives that guide action.

There is very little empirical work in support of the conscious position. DiMaggio (1991) and Brint and Karabel (1991) have made historical studies of the process of institutional creation among art museums and community colleges. They conclude that interested actors engaged in institutionalization projects to create the institutions they desired. In both studies (and in Davis and North 1971) institutions are created as the result of a political process. Almost everything about the institutionalization process remains to be explained, but at least this position can offer a prediction for the existence of organizational forms. To the extent that institutions influence organizational forms, the dominant organizational form will be the one favored by whoever can win the political process of establishing institutions.

ORGANIZATIONAL ECOLOGY

The final explanation I consider for the development of organizational forms is the most explicit. For organizational ecology the central question is how forms come to be represented on the organizational landscape. Hannan and Freeman (1989, 6) suggest that answering this question requires attention to the dynamics of organizational environments: "Exactly how does change in larger systems affect the forms of organizations in society?"

Ecologists have looked to effects on founding, mortality and change rates of organizations in order to understand the impact of environmental changes. "In other words, an ecology of organizations seeks to understand how social conditions affect the rates at which new organizations and new organizational forms arise, the rates at which organizations change forms, and the rates at which organizations and forms die out" (Hannan and Freeman 1989, 7). This interest in the rates of critical events that change organizational forms has resulted in much empirical work, mostly investigating founding and mortality rates of organizations (see Baum 1996 for a review).

The focus on founding and mortality processes results in explanations of changes in organizational populations that rely most heavily on selection. For selection to be a powerful influence it is necessary that organizations be inertial. Without some degree of inertia, organizations could effortlessly change to satisfy the environment: churches would turn into shoe stores overnight; large organizations would become small organizations; and organizations would never fail, or be founded.

How much inertia do organizations actually have? Well, as a beginning, they obviously have enough inertia for selection to operate, as evidenced by the numerous foundings and failures that occur every day. Inertial pressures are both internal and external to the organization. Internal pressures include investment in plant equipment and specialized personnel, limited information available to organizational decision makers, and internal politics. External pressures include legal and fiscal barriers, and legitimacy constraints. These pressures together are sufficiently compelling that structural inertia has been called "the most obvious feature of organizational life" (Hannan and Freeman 1977, 957).

While inertia seems obvious to some, it is controversial to others. The debate is about the importance of organizational history and environmental constraint versus strategic adaptation. Traditional views of management emphasize the role of adaptation (Hannan and Freeman 1989). In the adaptation argument, managers are considered capable of changing their organizations to meet the demands of the environment. All they need is the right theory, or strategy to tell them how their organizations should look. To the many theorists who see managers and organizations as capable of adaptation, organizational ecology seems deterministic. For these theorists, organizational ecology's emphasis on selection represents a disregard for human agency (e.g., Astley and Van de Ven 1983; Perrow 1986; Zucker 1989) or an understatement of the prevalence of organizational change (Young 1988).

Those who embrace strategic adaptation cite many instances of organizations that have successfully adjusted to their environments. To selectionists however, this is sampling on the dependent variable. It is not surprising that some organizations change successfully, what matters is that so many do not. For this reason empirical work on organizational ecology usually involves comprehensive data covering all members of a population over their complete existences. This analytic approach demonstrates the importance of selection despite managerial illusions of control. Typically, managers in every organization think that if have the "correct" strategy they will succeed, and they invariably use the strategy they think is correct. Yet, organizations with such managers fail every day. Even if adaptation is possible, neither managers nor adaptation theorists seem capable of predicting *a priori* what path will lead to success. When we examine aggregates of organizations, selection appears to operate without regard for managers' intentions to be strategic.

A full explanation of the rise of organizational forms, however, requires more than establishing the relevance of the environment. The question that remains unresolved is which forms will the environment select? Here is the opportunity for integrating the theories discussed so far. Efficiency and institutional congruence are critical dimensions which determine the success or failure of an organizational form. The environment selects organizations that are efficient, and those that satisfy institutional constraints.

But, because of the failings noted above of transaction cost and institutional theory, that observation is still insufficient. It is not enough to say the environment chooses efficient, institutionally congruent organizations, because we don't know where efficient alternatives, or institutional constraints come from. Organizational ecology attributes to the environment the power to determine organizational outcomes, but as long as the environment is treated as a black-box, those organizational outcomes are largely unexplained. This is disturbing because institutional and technical environments must obviously come from somewhere. It is even more disturbing because there are reasons to believe these environments are socially constructed; that they are affected by interested actors, perhaps the very same actors who operate the organizations that they affect. This is the theoretical problem this book addresses. I seek to develop a more complete view of the rise of organizational forms by considering the determinants of environments. Explaining the origin and change of organizational environments necessitates a focus on their critical technical and institutional elements.

2

The Creation and Change of Environments

Here I will describe an answer to the question "where do environments come from?" My claim is that the environments that organizations interact with are influenced by the organizations (and the entrepreneurs that operate them) themselves. Markets, dominant technologies and institutional rules are socially constructed. Rather than following some predetermined objective path these elements of the environment emerge at least partly through the interactions of interested actors. Manipulating institutional and technical environments is a strategy that entrepreneurs, organizations, and others use to improve their lot.

I will begin by considering arguments for and implications of interested actors affecting environments. Then I'll discuss the processes by which institutional and technical environments are manipulated. Finally, I'll outline the application of this argument to the population of hotel chains.

ACTORS AFFECTING ENVIRONMENTS

Organizational theorists have until recently said little about how environments change. In the 1960s it was necessary to argue that environments did in fact change. Work on the evolution of environments applied open systems theory to argue that environments were becoming more complex (Emery and Trist 1965; Terreberry 1968). However, few concrete details about the increasing complexity of environments are provided, and nothing is said about the causes of increasing environmental complexity, beyond that it results from increasing interdependence of components of the open system, and that it is beyond the control of any particular organization (they refer to environmental change processes as "autochthonous" [aboriginal or indigenous]). Despite their denial of agency as a cause of environmental change, an obvious extension of Emery and Trist's analysis suggests a role for agency. They identify four ideal types of environments, and for each outline an appropriate form of strategic action. Table 2–1 summarizes these types.

Table 2–1 shows that as environments progress in complexity, so do strategies. Placid, random environments require only an optimization tactic. Placid, clustered environments give a role to strategy because some locations are better than others. Disturbed-reactive environments add operations because of the necessity of incorporating the actions of competitors. The progression of complex strategies, however, stops there. The most complex environment, the turbulent field, is associated only with a number of coping strategies that respond to its uncertainty. The limited strategic responses to the turbulent environment result from Emery and Trist's contention that organizations cannot influence in any predictable way the changing environment. That contention is surely false. There are many obvious ways in which organizations affect their environments (Scott 1987b, 138). With the recognition of the reciprocal relationship between organizations and environments a new strategic option becomes available in turbulent environments: organizations can attempt to manipulate the environment.

Organizational ecologists have generally viewed environments as consistent with Emery and Trist's Type III or Type IV. They recognize that environments are dynamic, but treat environmental change as exogenous. Analyses of the interactions between sub-populations in different niches corresponds to the Type III environment. For example, Baum and Mezias (1992) find that the payoff to location, size and pricing strategies of Manhattan hotels depends on the strategies of other Manhattan hotels. Turbulent, Type IV environments are examined in Freeman and Hannan's (1983) analysis of niche widths of California restaurants. Variability and grain of environments determine the appropriateness of specialist and generalist strategies, but nothing is said about determinants of environmental variability.

The reciprocity between actors and environments has not been completely ignored by organizational ecologists. Hannan and Freeman (1989) describe a duality between organizational populations and environmental niches: niches define forms and forms define niches. The theory of density dependence (Hannan and Freeman 1987) argues that legitimacy and competition, which are elements of a given organization's environment, increase as the number of organizations in the population increases. Baum and Singh (1993) describe a "coevolution" between organizations and populations. All of these positions, however, describe non-

Table 2–1
Emery and Trist's (1965) Environmental Types and Implications for Strategy

Type	Description	Example	Appropriate Strategy
I. Placid, randomized.	Empty space, with randomly scattered bundles of resources.	Simon's (1957) idea of a surface over which an organism can locomote; Economist's classic market.	There is no distinction between tactics and strategy. The optimal strategy is doing one's best on a purely local basis.
II. Placid, clustered.	Goals and noxiants are not randomly distributed but hang together in certain ways.	The environment of an extractive industry; Economist's imperfect competition.	Strategy becomes separate from tactics. Survival is linked to what organization knows of its environment.
III. Disturbed-reactive.	A Type II environment in which there are more than one organization of the same kind.	Economist's oligopolic market.	Operations are introduced: campaigns involving planned series of tactical initiatives, calculated reactions by others, and counter-actions.
IV. Turbulent field.	Dynamic processes arise from the field itself.	Modern industries.	Responses to uncertainty such as "organizational matrices."

strategic relationships between actors and environments and all except the theory of density dependence focus on the interactions between an organizational form and other types of organizations in the environment. This view of the environment as made up of non-strategic relationships with other forms is consistent with biological models of inter-population competition (and consistent with Emery and Trist 1965 and Terreberry 1968).

While I agree that direct and indirect competition is important for the evolution of organizations, my approach is based on the fact that the environments faced by organizations are more intricate than those faced by biological organisms. Organizations can be affected by competitive (or mutualistic) relationships with other types of organizations, but they are also affected by ideas, norms and laws. The origin and effect of these elements of the environment are my focus. After all, the effect the Federal government has on the population of small businesses would not be adequately captured by modeling the number of Federal government offices. Pfeffer and Salancik (1978) have discussed the strategic action of managers and entrepreneurs to manipulate the ideas, norms and laws that are part of the organizational environment. They claim that "managers not only adapt their organizations to the context, but may take actions to modify the environment to which the organization then responds" (266–267). The position that I present here is captured with a restatement of that passage to reflect the importance of selection: environments select organizations, but managers and entrepreneurs may take actions to modify the environment which determines their success or failure.

The above statement of my argument presents starkly what may seem like an incongruity with past work in organizational ecology. Clearly, I am giving an important role to managerial action. Is this a "back-door" for the adaptationist perspective? Am I claiming that rather than change their organizations to fit the environment, Herculean managers simply change the environment to fit their organizations? No. As I explain below, manipulating environments is a complicated, largely political endeavor. Many actors pursue their interests by attempting to manipulate the environment. Many of the interests they pursue are conflicting. The resulting interactions could be described as a "war of interests," and the winners will be those that can muster the most power in support of their cause. I expect that failure in attempts to manipulate the environment is common. There are, however, strategies for changing the environment that have been demonstrated as successful.

Which Organizations Will Actors Champion?

If environments are partly the result of efforts of actors to affect them, then the first question to ask is, in which directions will actors try to manipulate the environment? The short answer is that they will try to manipulate the environment to serve their interests. Of course, non-tautological theory requires *a priori* identification of these interests. Here efficiency theories are useful. Assuming entrepreneurs are free to choose the form of their organization before it is founded, they will desire to operate organizations that they perceive to be more efficient than alternatives.

Efficiency is partly socially determined, such as with the establishment of a technological standard, which often depends on perception and social processes as much as objective efficiency, but there are also elements of efficiency that persist across negotiated environments. First, there are natural laws that govern the behavior of matter. For instance, one design for a flour mill may be preferred by gravity over another. Second, while not natural laws, there are some extremely well supported generalizations about animal behavior. An organizational structure that rewarded employees for exerting effort would be more efficient than one that didn't. Third, there are elements of technical and institutional environments that are sufficiently stable during an organizational life as to be treated as constant. An organization in the U.S. designed to be congruent with a capitalist system would be more efficient than one designed to be congruent with a socialist system.

The championing of organizations with perceived efficiency advantages will, under simple assumptions, result in substantial support for organizational forms with actual efficiency advantages. Following Scharfstein and Stein (1990), imagine that there are entrepreneurs with guesses at what is efficient and entrepreneurs with no guesses. Among those with guesses, some are right and will amass in support of the efficient form, and some are wrong and will support a random form. Those with no guesses can take advantage of the information of others by "following the herd" and supporting the form that most others support. As long as there are a reasonably large number of inefficient forms that those with bad guesses may randomly choose to support, the efficient form will have significantly greater support than any alternative. It will have the support of all entrepreneurs with good guesses, and all entrepreneurs with no guesses.

Of course, entrepreneurs may not always be free to choose their organizations. It could be that entrepreneurs are "endowed" with an organizational form and must operate it or nothing; or past investments may cause entrepreneurs to favor a sub-optimal form. For example, when a family firm passes to the second generation the inheritors are not free to choose a new industry, strategy, or location. Whether their organizational forms are chosen because of perceived efficiency, or because of endowments, entrepreneurs' and managers' interests depend on the success of their organizations, and they will try to manipulate the environment to favor them.

Manipulating Institutional Environments

DiMaggio (1988) offers the term "institutional entrepreneurs" to describe actors that pursue their interests by manipulating institutional rules. He claims that creating new legitimate organizational forms—such as universities, art museums or hotel chains—requires an "institutionalization project." Such projects may require the strength of many actors, and part of the task of institutional entrepreneurs is to build necessary coalitions. DiMaggio (1991) describes an institutionalization project to reform U.S. art museums. The institutional entrepreneurs in this case were university trained professional employees and they coopted actors such as the Carnegie Commission in order to promote their concept of the role of the art museum.

North (1990) notes that organizations will try to influence the polity as a means to manipulate institutional rules. However, North's most important insight regarding the interactions between actors and institutions concerns the path dependence of institutional rules. He recognizes that the institutional framework provides the incentives that guide action, and that actors will respond to the incentives provided by the institutional framework *regardless of the efficiency of that framework*. So, even if institutional rules are sub-optimal there will be some actors who are favored by them, and who can be expected to defend them. This built-in defense causes institutional frameworks to be path dependent. Radical changes are more difficult because interests in the current institutional framework always oppose interests in institutional change.

Manipulating Technical Environments

Actors can contribute to technical change by providing innovations, and encouraging the diffusion of innovations. A healthy debate exists regarding the source of innovations, with the central question being whether innovations are mainly knowledge-induced or demand-induced. My argument that strategic action is an important determinant of environments implies that innovations should be mainly demand-induced. In his classic *Invention and Economic Growth* (1966), Schmookler supports the demand-induced position. His conclusions are based partly on the observation that inventions in two or more different technologies used in the same industry, such as railroad track and non-track inventions, follow very similar temporal patterns. Because different technologies in the same industry have different knowledge bases, but highly correlated demands, similarity in temporal patterns of invention supports the claim that it is the value and not the cost of invention that is dominant.

Podolny and Stuart (1994) suggest that technological diffusion depends partly on the status of firms associated with innovations. In a study of technological change in the semiconductor industry they find that the citations of a patent depend on the status and market presence of organizations already using the technology represented by that patent. High status actors attract others to the technologies they use and in that way have high power to cause technological change. Granovetter (1991) makes a compatible argument to explain the creation of the dominant standard in electricity generation. There were viable alternatives (such as generating electricity on site at homes and businesses) to the system of central generators and transmission of electricity to users. Granovetter attributes the outcome to the personal networks of a few individuals. Thomas Edison and his personal secretary Samuel Insull used connections to financiers, political leaders and inventors to outmaneuver J.P. Morgan and others who favored local generation. "Edison won the battle not because his solution was the technologically correct one, but rather because he was able to construct winning coalitions of key actors" (14).

Empirical Evidence of the Manipulation of Environments

Evidence in support of the arguments made here can be of three types. First, there is evidence that organizations act consciously to manipulate the environment. This could consist of statistical tests for certain behaviors or structures of organizations. I analyzed the influences on having someone whose job it was to manipulate government policy in a random sample of organizations from Minnesota (Ingram 1993a). Government policy is a salient element of the institutional environment, and the arguments I have made above suggest that the stronger the interests that organizations represent, the more likely they will be to try to influence government policy. I operationalized the strength of interest that the organization represents with the number or participants in the organization, and its income. Both these variables increased the likelihood of having someone whose job it is to manipulate government policy.

A second type of evidence comes from comparing the features of the environment to the strengths of actors who are affected by it. The expectation would be that the environment will conform to the most powerful interests. Under some circumstances, interests and environments can be operationalized with enough cross-sectional or longitudinal variance to perform a statistical analysis. Stigler (1971) analyzed laws regarding weight limits on trucks in the early 1930's. Weight limits on trucks were hotly contested because they were critical to the competitiveness of trucks against the railroads. Stigler predicts that states with many trucks on farms (X1 below) would have higher limits due to demands of agriculture interests; states where the average length of rail hauls (X2) is higher would have higher limits because trucks compete more with short rail hauls than long ones; and states with better road surfaces (X3) would have higher limits because of lower damage risks from heavy trucks. Table 2–2 shows a regression analysis that supports all his predictions. A positive coefficient for one of the explanatory variables (X1, X2 or X3) indicates that higher levels of that variable result in higher weight limits for trucks. For example, the coefficient for X1 in the first regression indicates that an increase of one unit in the number of trucks on farms (which X1 represents) results in an increase of 0.034 units in the predicted weight limit for four-wheel trucks.

Table 2–2
Regression Analysis of State Weight Limits on Trucks
Stigler (1971)

Dependent Variable	N	Constant	X1	X2	X3
Limit: Four-Wheel Trucks	48	12.28	0.034	0.028	0.264
		(4.87)	(3.99)	(2.77)	(3.0)
Limit: Six-Wheel Trucks	46	10.34	0.044	0.079	0.253
		(1.57)	(2.01)	(2.97)	(1.1)

(t values in parentheses)

The third type of evidence, the one I rely on most heavily in this book, is to document the history of the features of a certain environment. History is the only reasonable alternative to analyze a single environment where there is no cross-sectional variance, and variables such as the actions of various interest groups across time are not quantifiable. Another advantage of historical analysis is that it can provide insight into causality that statistical analysis often cannot. For example, Van de Ven and Garud (1993) statistically analyze technical developments in Cochlear Implants by analyzing the temporal relationship between institutional and technical change. They find that technical changes often follow institutional changes, and conclude that the institutional environment is an important driver of technical change. The same type of analysis on hotel chain control systems would find that industry acceptance of the NCR front office posting machine (a technical change) followed its inclusion in the curriculum of Cornell's hotel school (an institutional change). Enough events like that would lead to statistical support of Van de Ven and Garud's assertion about the relationship between institutional and technical environments. However, a historical analysis leads to a different conclusion. The use of the NCR posting machine at Cornell was caused by Statler Hotels. E.M. Statler was involved in the design of the posting machine, and to promote its diffusion he arranged for equipment and training to be given to Cornell. It seems that Statler ultimately changed the technical environment, and the change in the institutional environment was merely instrumental.

Although in the above example statistical analysis identifies a proximate cause while historical analysis avoids that trap, it is often historical analysis that identifies proximate causes. Further, historical analysis can suffer from biases in the historical record and biases of the investigator. For these reasons, it is complemented by evidence of the first two types described above. If we know that organizations act politically, and that environments reflect political activity, then a historic account of political activities around a particular environment is defensible. Further, the theory I have outlined provides guide posts for a good historical analysis of environmental change. It suggests that there should be competing groups trying to influence the environment. Identification and consideration of these groups is necessary. Further, there are generalizable claims about what makes one group more powerful or effective politically than another. These claims can be applied to explain the outcomes of a historical case.

Finally, while in many cases explaining a particular environment requires historical analysis, explaining the effects of the environment does not. All of the methodological techniques of organizational ecology can be used in the framework I have outlined. Once the causes of the environment are understood, the effects of the environment on organizational mortality, founding, and change can be statistically analyzed. In fact, the analysis of environmental effects provides a final test of my theory. If environments are created by actors pursuing their interests, then the winners of political battles should find their organizations favored by selection. The champions identified by the historical and statistical analyses should be the same.

SUMMARY

I have argued that environments are affected by actors trying to advantage themselves or their organizations. Actors will act on behalf of organizational forms that they favor because of perceived efficiency, or because of endowments or sunk costs. They may attempt to manipulate the environment in a number of ways such as building coalitions or using coercion. The environment thus determined selects organizations and causes the growth or decline of organizational forms.

Application to the Population of Hotel Chains

The remainder of this book applies the argument that entrepreneurs affect environments to favor their organizations to explain the rise of hotel chains in the U.S. I will describe two efficiency advantages that caused entrepreneurs to favor hotel chains over independently owned hotels. They are economies of scale, and the ability to develop reputations through repeated interactions. I will discuss why these are advantages for hotel chains in chapter 3.

I will focus on the creation of institutions that provide a supply of professional managers as a manipulation of the institutional environment that favored hotel chains. In chapter 4, I will discuss the political battles between chain entrepreneurs and the operators of independent hotels that resulted in university programs to educate hotel managers.

The change in the technical environment I will describe is the creation of control systems that solved agency problems faced by chains. No group strongly opposed the creation of these systems, but I will describe the efforts of chain entrepreneurs to create and promote them in chapter 5.

I begin the statistical analysis that demonstrates the presence of efficiency advantages of chains, and the effects of environmental manipulations with a description of data and analytic strategy in chapter 6. Chapter 7 is an analysis of chain mortality, chapter 8 is an analysis of chain founding and chapter 9 is an analysis of chain growth and decline. Chapter 10 presents a test to show that the same environmental manipulations that helped chains hurt independent hotels. A discussion and conclusion is presented in chapter 11.

Figure 2–1 illustrates the interaction of agency and environment to cause a change in the form of organization in the hotel industry. The left-most box of the figure shows the strategic opportunities of hotel chains as initial conditions. These strategic opportunities induce entrepreneurs to act on behalf of the chain form of organization. In other words, because chains offer the potential of economies of scale and repeated interactions with guests, entrepreneurs see a strategic advantage from operating chains and try to change the environment so that hotel chains are easier to operate. The changes to the institutional environment and technical environment that make chains easier to operate are shown in the two boxes in the middle of the figure. Strategic opportunities, change in the institutional environment, and change in the technical environment all contribute to the evolution from owner-operated hotels to hotel chains. These causal relationships are indicated by the arrows to the right-most box from the other three boxes.

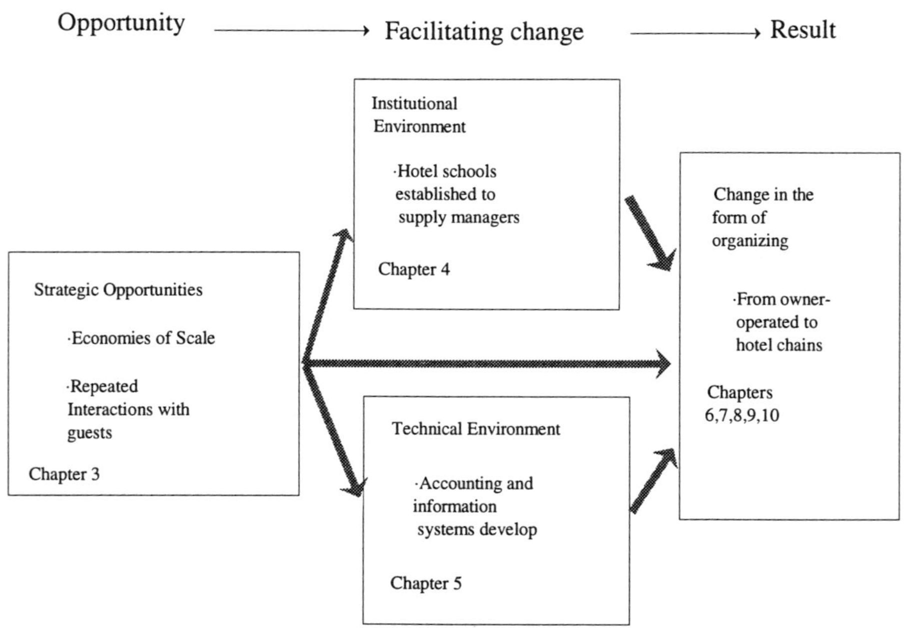

Figure 2-1. Application of Argument to Hotel Chains.

3

Advantages of Hotel Chains

In this chapter I describe the advantages of hotel chains that made the chain form of organization appealing to entrepreneurs, and prompted them to attempt to change institutional and technical environments to facilitate the operation of hotel chains. The advantages are economies of scale, and the ability to engage in repeated interactions with customers by linking the units of a chain together with common names.

ECONOMIES OF SCALE

As a 1938 advertisement from the *Hotel Red Book* summarizes, "the chain represents efficiency, economical management, savings in the purchase of supplies and other phases of scientific operation." Economies of scale are one of the advantages chains have over independent hotels. Central purchasing results in significant cost savings for hotel chains (Kerley 1949). The savings result because hotel chains can purchase furniture, linen, food and other supplies in larger quantities than independent hotels can. Sometimes, the scale of operations of hotel chains allows them to have items such as furniture custom made. Economies of scale are also possible in advertising, reservation systems, and cash management (Caraux 1976). Larger hotel chains will benefit most from economies of scale.

I will represent the economy of scale argument, and the other arguments that are at the theoretical core of this book in hypothesis form for easy reference. A hypothesis is a concise statement of the form "as X increases (or decreases) Y will increase (or decrease)" which serves to link the theoretical claims made in the first half of this book to the empirical tests on the evolution of hotel chains that are presented in the second half. The economy of scale argument outlines an advantage for larger chains, which should result in larger chains being favored by selection. Organizations that are favored by selection pressures should be expected, among other things, to have lower rates of mortality.

Hypothesis 1a: The mortality risk of a hotel chain will decrease as the size of the chain increases.

Economies of scale will be greater for chains that are geographically concentrated. Mass purchasing and advertising is easier when the units of an organization are close to each other. For example, if a chain makes mass purchases of meat from a single wholesaler, it must then deliver the meat to its hotels. If the hotels are geographically concentrated the cost of delivery will be less. Even if the wholesaler handles the delivery, the cost of delivery will be factored into the cost of the meat and will be less if the hotels are geographically concentrated. Savings of this type for the many products a chain purchases will result in significant cost advantages for geographically concentrated chains. These cost advantages will make geographically concentrated chains less likely to fail.

Hypothesis 1b: The mortality risk of a hotel chain will decrease as the geographic concentration of its hotels increases.

THE AUTOMOBILE AGE AND DISCONTENT WITH INDEPENDENT HOTELS

The advent of the automobile meant important changes in the travel patterns of Americans which meant changes for American hotels. Leisure travel was revolutionized. The automobile democratized holiday travel, bringing it within reach of the masses. The families that had always traveled were no longer fated to holiday at seaside resort hotels. In the early 1900s it became possible and increasingly common to enjoy an automotive adventure across the country. Some hoteliers felt they were ideally positioned to take advantage of this change, and in fact encouraged it. Hotel associations in the west spent much of the first three decades of this century rallying around a "See America First" promotion movement.

However, the expected boom for hotels did not materialize. Rather, the increasing exposure of Americans to hotels infected the population with a dissatisfaction with hotels. It is difficult to imagine given the consumerism of American business since 1950, but hotels in the early part of the century seemed unwilling or unable to accommodate the desires of their customers.

Tourists were greeted in the small town hotel by interiors typically unchanged since the 1870s; an obstacle course of greedy waiters, clerks and bellhops demanding tips and offering hostile service; bad food; and oppressive schedules, atmosphere and dress codes (Belasco 1979, 44–56). Seaside resorts tended to be a little less seedy, but just as oppressive, with three changes of clothing required each day to meet the demands of hotel etiquette. Hotels were particularly un-welcoming to auto tourists, who were ashamed to walk through the hotel lobby in their dirty road clothes. Representative is the impression of Claire Boltwood, heroine of Sinclair Lewis's semi-autobiographical novel *Free Air* (1919, 259) upon arriving at the only good hotel in Gopher Prairie: "In the hotel Claire was conscious of the ugliness of the poison-green walls and brass cuspidors and insurance calendars and bare floor of the office; conscious of the interesting scientific fact that all air had been replaced by the essence of cigar smoke and cooking cabbage; of the stares of the traveling men lounging in bored lines; and of the lack of welcome on the part of the night clerk, an oldish bleached man with whiskers instead of a collar."

Their dissatisfaction caused travelers to look for alternatives to hotels. Of course they could decide not to travel, or arrange trips so they could stay with relatives. But the most interesting alternative that developed was the autocamping movement. Compelled by dissatisfaction with hotels and the constraints of rail travel, and a desire for the freedom of a "gypsy," Americans began camping out of their automobiles. The autocampers would tour the country in their cars, sometimes pulling a trailer. They would buy food along the roadside and in the evenings set up camp, either alone in a field or with others in an established autocamping site. Estimates of the number of autocampers between 1920 and 1925 ranged from ten to twenty million each year (Belasco 1979). Autocamping was also popular across class boundaries. One 1921 trip included President Harding, Thomas Edison and Henry Ford.

Initially autocampers would set up camp in any convenient location. Often in farmers' fields, but also in school yards and other open spaces. Understandably, this became unacceptable as autocamping moved from a fad to an institution. Farmers and others experienced rampant trespassing, vandalism, and thievery. The campers themselves were at risk because their inexperience exposed them to many diseases. Municipalities responded to these problems by establishing and subsidizing free autocamps "to keep tourists and natives separate, and to protect tourists from themselves" (Belasco 1979, 76). Originally open spaces with some kind of latrine, these camps grew more elaborate as municipalities competed to attract tourists.

Running water and cabins became the norm. Roadside camps were privatized and evolved into the present day motel. The small town hoteliers left behind by this movement would empathize with the proprietor of the local hotel in Sherwood Anderson's *Winesburg, Ohio*, (1947, 25) who, looking back at his failing property cursed "damn such a life, damn it!"

GAME THEORY ON THE LIABILITY OF INDEPENDENT HOTELS AND THE SOLUTION OF CHAINS

Game theory is a field of mathematics that is commonly applied to analyze economic interactions. The game theoretic approach is to formally analyze the interactions between actors (referred to as players). The set of actions available to each player is identified, the likely actions of opposing players are considered, the implications of a player's actions in the context of likely responses of opponents are calculated, and in this way the action that best serves the player's interests can be identified. The benefit of the approach is that it illuminates the complexities of strategic behavior. For many interactions it is not possible to casually determine which action best serves an individual. Within assumptions, game theory is useful for solving this problem.

Here I'll use game theory to demonstrate why independent hotels should have experienced the difficulty satisfying customers that they did, and how chains avoid the problem. For simplicity I'll consider two possible actions for each the hotel and customer. The hotel can provide good service (this move symbolized by δ), or bad service (β). The customer can stay at the hotel (α), or find an alternative such as autocamping (γ). I'll use the following symbols to represent one-shot payoffs of utility (utility describes an abstract measure of benefit to the actor) for each action:

δ_α = payoff to hotel if hotel provides good service and customer stays;
δ_γ = payoff to hotel if hotel provides good service and customer doesn't stay;
β_α = payoff to hotel if hotel provides bad service and customer stays;
β_γ = payoff to hotel if hotel provides bad service and customer doesn't stay;
α_δ = payoff to customer if customer stays and hotel has good service;
α_β = payoff to customer if customer stays and hotel has bad service;
γ_δ = payoff to customer if customer doesn't stay and hotel has good service;

γ_β = payoff to customer if customer doesn't stay and hotel has bad service.

Although I am using symbols for generalizability, there are relationships that must logically hold between the payoffs. For the hotel:

(3–1) $\delta_\alpha > \delta_\gamma$, $\delta_\alpha > \beta_\gamma$, $\beta_\alpha > \beta_\gamma$ and $\beta_\alpha > \delta_\gamma$ because the hotel always prefers to have a customer stay than not stay. This is because hotels have high fixed costs, so even if they are not profitable, and even if they provide good service (with high marginal cost), marginal revenues exceed marginal costs for an additional customer.

(3–2) $\beta_\alpha > \delta_\alpha$ and $\beta_\gamma > \delta_\gamma$ because it is cheaper to provide bad service than good service.

By transitivity, the ordering of the hotel's preferences are $\beta_\alpha > \delta_\alpha > \beta_\gamma > \delta_\gamma$. For the customer:

(3–3) $\alpha_\delta > \alpha_\beta$ because it is better to stay at a hotel with good service than one with bad service.

(3–4) $\gamma_\delta = \gamma_\beta$ because the customer is indifferent between a good hotel and a bad hotel when not staying there.

(3–5) $\alpha_\delta > \gamma_\delta = \gamma_\beta$ because there is no evidence that customers' tastes have changed such that they do not want a hotel regardless of the quality. Revealed preference shows that a good hotel is preferable to the alternatives.

(3–6) $\alpha_\beta < \gamma_\delta = \gamma_\beta$ because revealed preference (historical trends described above) shows that customers do prefer alternatives to a bad hotel.

By transitivity the ordering of the customer's preferences are $\alpha_\delta > \gamma_\delta = \gamma_\beta > \alpha_\beta$.

In many if not most cases, the interaction between a customer and a stand alone hotel will be a "one-shot" encounter. Most travelers do not return to the same city with great frequency[1]. They may not return to a city or town for years, so there is little chance that they can offer a hotel important business in the future. This in turn effects the incentive of the hotel to offer good service. On many dimensions it is difficult for travelers to tell if a hotel will provide a good stay until they register, move their bags in, try the television, ice machine, and shower, and send out their dry cleaning. By this time, it is too late to change hotels. So, the hotel has no reason to excel on the dimensions that are not apparent before the customer registers. If the bed is too soft, or the ice machine broken, the customer will go away unhappy but since no future business was forthcoming from that customer, no harm is done to the hotel. The historical account above describes the customer's response to this incentive structure. Bad experiences with hotels came to be expected, and alternatives to staying at hotels were developed.

The problems that arise from the interrelation of the payoffs of a traveler and a hotel can be systematically demonstrated by analyzing the interaction between customer and hotel as a simple one-shot, simultaneous-move game[2]. The payoffs described above are related to each other in this matrix, which shows the moves available to the hotel and the customer, and the payoffs resulting from interactions of those moves:

		Hotel	
		Good Service (δ)	Bad Service (β)
Customer	Stay at Hotel (α)	α_δ, δ_α	α_β, β_α
	Don't Stay at Hotel (γ)	γ_δ, δ_γ	γ_β, β_γ

Figure 3–1. Payoff Matrix of One-Shot Encounter Between Customer and Hotel.

The relationships between these payoffs can be used to determine a unique solution for the game, called a "Nash equilibrium." The process is to determine what move a player prefers for each possible move made by the opponent. So, for the hotel, I first determine what is preferred if the customer stays at a hotel. By (3–2), $\beta_\alpha > \delta_\alpha$, so β_α is preferred, and is underlined in Figure 3–2. If the customer doesn't stay, then the hotel prefers β_γ, again by (3–2). For the customer, α_δ is preferable if the hotel has good service according to (3–5). γ_β is preferable if the hotel has bad service according to (3–6). Figure 3–2 indicates that when the hotel offers bad service and the customer does not stay at the hotel neither player can get a higher payoff by choosing a different move. This intersection of actions where neither player can improve their outcome with a different action is Nash equilibrium of the game.

		Hotel	
		Good Service (δ)	Bad Service (β)
Customer	Stay at Hotel (α)	$\underline{\alpha}_\delta$, δ_α	α_β, $\underline{\beta}_\alpha$
	Don't Stay at Hotel (γ)	γ_δ, δ_γ	$\underline{\gamma}_\beta$, $\underline{\beta}_\gamma$

Figure 3–2. Nash Equilibrium of One-Shot Encounter Between Customer and Hotel.

This game is different from the famous prisoner's dilemma because "defection" is not always preferred by a player to "cooperation," since the customer would stay at the hotel if he or she knew that the service would be good. However, the mutually dissatisfying result is the same. The ordering of preferences above shows that both players would prefer a situation where the hotel offers good service and the customer stays at the hotel. They cannot achieve it because of the structure of their interaction.

Since the Nash equilibrium of the one-shot encounter is sub-optimal for both the hotel and customer, we would expect that there would be attempts to change the structure of the encounter. Customers tried to do this by attempting to determine the quality of a hotel before they checked in. They would ask to see all the rooms and would "bounce on the beds" (Belasco 1979). However, this is not a good solution to the problem because such demonstrations of quality are costly in effort for the hotel and the customer, and many features of a hotel are not as easy to demonstrate as the quality of the furnishings. Some hotels built model rooms (some were even designed like store fronts, so potential customers could examine them without leaving their cars) to evidence their quality, but this does not solve the problem because the model room may not represent the room the customer is assigned to.

A better solution could be achieved by hotel chains. Because of their multiple locations hotel chains can have repeated, rather than one-shot encounters with customers. Even if the customer never visits the same city twice he or she will have many opportunities to patronize a large chain. Similarly, the customer can tell friends about the chain because they too are likely to encounter it on their travels. If a customer has a pleasant stay at the

Holiday Inn at Memphis, the Holiday Inn at Little Rock will get more business. A customer can be more confident that a large chain will provide good service because the chain has an incentive to encourage future patronage. This interpretation is supported by a 1936 advertisement for the American Hotel Corporation that claimed "the manager is thinking not only of himself and his hotel. He is thinking of the good name of *every other hotel in the system* (emphasis in original)."

Game theorists call the fact that repeated interactions can generate multiple equilibria the "folk theorem" because it was widely known before it was published (Gibbons 1992). It is a simple matter to demonstrate that under reasonable conditions one of the equilibria for the repeated interaction of customers and hotels is that the hotel provides good service and the customer stays at the hotel. First, recognize that repeated interactions between a customer and a chain occur with some probability, but are not certain. Customers die or stop traveling and hotel chains stop operating. Second, the value of a payoff some time in the future is less than the value of the same payoff today. So the value of future interactions must be discounted. The discount factor of a certain payoff one year in the future is its value divided by (1 + r) where r is the interest rate or more generally the time value of payoffs. If the payoff is uncertain then its discounted value must be multiplied by (1 - p) where p is the probability that the relationship will stop after the current interaction. So the appropriate discount factor, τ, is:

$$\tau = \frac{1-p}{1+r} . \qquad (3\text{–}7)$$

A payoff n periods in the future is discounted n times. The present value of the infinite sequence of payoffs π_1, π_2, π_3,.... is:

$$\pi_1 + \tau\pi_2 + \tau^2\pi_3 \ldots = \sum_{t=1}^{\infty} \tau^{t-1}\pi_t . \qquad (3\text{–}8)$$

Now, what if the customer has a strategy to stay at the hotel in the current period, and in every subsequent period as long as the service is good, but to never go to the hotel again if the service is bad in any period. The general class of strategies similar to this are called "trigger" strategies because one defection on the part of the other player triggers an infinite reprisal from the focal player. Facing this strategy the hotel has two options. It can offer good service, and obtain δ_α indefinitely (as the game is, if it is worthwhile to offer good service in the current period, it will be worthwhile in every future period), for which the present value would be:

$$\delta_\alpha + \tau\cdot\delta_\alpha + \tau^2\cdot\delta_\alpha + \ldots = \frac{\delta_\alpha}{1-\tau} . \qquad (3\text{–}9)$$

Alternatively the hotel could offer bad service. For one period the hotel would get β_α because the customer would stay, and for every other period the hotel would get β_γ because the customer would never return. The present value would be:

$$\beta_\alpha + \tau\cdot\beta_\gamma + \tau^2\cdot\beta_\gamma + \ldots = \beta_\alpha + \frac{\tau\cdot\beta_\gamma}{1-\tau} . \qquad (3\text{–}10)$$

The hotel will choose to offer good service when the present value expressed in (3–9) is greater than the present value expressed in (3–10):

$$\frac{\delta_\alpha}{1-\tau} > \beta_\alpha + \frac{\tau\cdot\beta_\gamma}{1-\tau} , \qquad (3\text{–}11)$$

or:

$$\tau > \frac{\beta_\alpha - \delta_\alpha}{\beta_\alpha - \beta_\gamma} . \qquad (3\text{–}12)$$

The hotel's preferences described above showed that $\beta_\alpha > \delta_\alpha > \beta_\gamma$, so (3–12) indicates a necessary value of τ between 0 and 1 for the hotel to offer good service (remember as τ approaches 1 future payoffs are more important). The relationship expressed in (3–12) is intuitively appealing. The more important future business is (i.e., the greater τ is) the more likely the hotel is to offer good service. The larger the payoff to tricking the customer by providing bad service during the current period (β_α), the more important future business must be to justify good service (the right side of [3–12] approaches 1 as β_α increases). The greater the payoff for providing good service to a customer who stays (δ_α) the less important future business must be to justify good service (the right side of [3–12] approaches 0 as δ_α approaches β_α). The greater the payoff for providing bad service when the customer does not stay (β_γ) the more important future business must be to justify good service (the right side of [3–12] approaches 1 as β_γ approaches δ_α).

Typically in demonstrations of a repeated-game equilibrium, derivation of the conditions for which the equilibrium holds for one player is followed by a similar derivation for the other player, but such a derivation is unnecessary here. As noted above, the customer prefers the payoff for staying at a hotel with good service (α_δ) to all other payoffs. So, if the customer is confident that the hotel will offer good service (i.e., if the conditions set out in (3–12) are met) he or she will stay at the hotel. The customer has no incentive to defect from the arrangement where the hotel offers good service and the customer patronizes the hotel.

The above analysis shows how a mutually preferable equilibrium is possible when the hotel organization is capable of repeated encounters with a customer. Of course, that equilibrium would not hold if the customer was incapable of repeated encounters with the hotel organization. Some customers travel extremely infrequently, or for some reason may be almost certain to never travel again. Even these customers can be important to a hotel chain's future because they probably know someone who will have an opportunity to patronize the chain, and they can tell this person about the quality of the service they received. So, while the analysis deals explicitly with the history of the relationship between a customer and a chain, it can be generalized to include the hotel's reputation as a potential customer is aware of it. Only customers who can't stay with the chain again, and who know no one who can, are truly unimportant to the chain's future. When interacting with these customers hotels would maximize their payoffs by providing bad service. However, it is difficult for hotels to identify the likelihood that any particular customer falls into this category. Therefore, customers who won't have the opportunity to bring further business can free ride on the importance of those who will. Hotel chains can adjust the rate they use to discount future payoffs to account for the fact that some customers have no possibility of bringing future business.

Application to Naming Strategies

There is one more step necessary before I can provide a hypothesis regarding the repeated-interaction argument. For a chain to benefit from the ability of repeated interactions to create an equilibrium where the customer expects good service and stays at the hotel, it is necessary that the customer recognize that various units are part of the same chain. The only way this is possible is if the units are named in some fashion that allows them to be associated with each other. Therefore, chains that give more of their units the same name will have greater repeated-interaction advantages, and will be less likely to fail.

Hypothesis 2: The mortality risk of a hotel chain will decrease as the proportion of its hotels with the same name increases.

Given the arguments I have presented it may be unclear why any chain would not give all of its units the same name and take full advantage of repeated-interaction opportunities. Some chains simply had different ideas about what constituted an effective naming strategy. In fact, the largest chain in the first half of the twentieth century, United Hotels run by Frank Dudley, gave all units idiosyncratic names. This was partly due to Dudley's belief that "a hotel was primarily a community center, which should reflect the cultural heritage of that community as well as the financial investment of some of its citizens" (American Hotel and Motel Association (AHMA) Archives VI, 106). United built almost all of its units (rather than buying old units which already had established names), and was like other chains except in its naming strategy. It is left to the test of the effect of naming strategy on mortality to determine whether the strategic advantage of common names I have described, or Dudley's strategy of local identification of units, was more effective.

4

Institutional Change: The Supply of Professional Managers

A critical difference between hotel chains and independent hotels is the reliance on professional managers. Hotel chains could not flourish until a supply of these managers was established. Establishing this supply required manipulation of institutional rules: the rules governing education became the subject of a political battle between early hotel chain operators and other interested actors. Eventually, the hotel chain faction was able to establish degree programs in hospitality management at universities. These programs supplied the managerial resources that hotel chains required. This chapter documents and analyzes this case of institutional change.

Following North (1990) institutions are seen here as social rules, of which actors are aware and respond to strategically. The contribution of hotel school education to the hotel chain form of organization can also be seen in a different institutional light. DiMaggio and Powell (1983) argue that professionalization is a source of normative isomorphism, compelling organizations to adopt a common form. There are two aspects of professionalization that are relevant for this purpose. First, professions legitimate a cognitive base produced by university specialists; second, professions promote the establishment of professional networks that span organizations and across which innovations diffuse rapidly. So, the professional managers in hospitality that hotel schools create may legitimate the hotel chain organizational form. Such managers share a knowledge base built on the assumption that general management principles can be applied to hotels, and they form a network across which ideas about organizational structure can diffuse.

THE LABOR PROBLEM IN THE U.S. HOSPITALITY INDUSTRY

Complaints of a shortage of labor were one of the most common topics of discussion at gatherings of hoteliers in the early part of the twentieth century (AHMA Archives). The rapid growth of the industry combined with the lack of a training system for hotel employees created this problem (Inman 1993). The outbreak of World War I made the problem critical. Previous to that, the largest hotel organizations had relied on employees trained in European hotel schools, and in the apprenticeship system of European hospitality to fill minor executive roles. These employees also provided training for subordinates (AHMA Archives, IV 70). In 1914 many of these employees returned to Europe, and the supply of well trained immigrants dried up.

After the war the crisis continued. New U.S. immigration policies made it much more difficult for Europeans to enter the country. In New York the labor problem was so severe that there were calls for the New York City Hotel Association to use its influence to get the immigration restrictions eased (AHMA Archives, VI 27). When European employees could be acquired they were now less valuable because of suspicion generated by the "Red scare." In fact one hotel chain, the Boomer-Dupont System in New York City, went so far as to require foreign employees "to study 'Americanism' and to wear red, white, and blue ribbons, as an answer to the 'Bolsheviks' and other undesirable aliens" (AHMA Archives, VI 29).

Although the entire hospitality industry suffered from this shortage of labor, the problem was worse for early hotel chains. In 1918 there were twenty-five hotel chains, and these organizations needed not only the traditional hotel employees, but also a new type of hotel employee: the professional manager. Hotel chains are an example of the modern business enterprise which has management by a hierarchy of salaried executives as a defining characteristic (Chandler 1977, 1). Hotel chains are (typically) larger and more geographically disperse than independent hotels. This introduces a number of activities that are necessary for the success of a hotel chain. Training and personnel practices, planning and coordination, and control are important for the success of a hotel chain. Hotel chains must be "managed," as opposed to merely operated.

Alternative Solutions to the Labor Problem

There are four groups who might reasonably be expected to pay for the training of employees in an industry: the state, the industry, the organizations and the employees themselves (Ingram 1997). The industry or the state could establish a centralized training system, and this is ultimately what happened in the U.S. hotel industry, with the industry providing financial support. The balance of this chapter deals with this system and its creation. Before that analysis, I will briefly discuss why two alternative systems were not adopted. The first alternative was an apprentice system which puts the cost of training on the employee. The second alternative was for organizations to absorb the cost of training by establishing in-house training programs.

In the European hospitality industry the apprentice system was used with great success. The European employees who were the foundation of the American hospitality industry prior to World War I were trained in that system, so obviously it was capable of providing qualified employees at that time. The evidence, while not conclusive, seems to indicate that the apprentice system was a victim of the isolationist sentiment that seized the United States after World War I. In a 1936 letter to a European hotel educator, Dean Howard Meek of Cornell's hotel school claimed that apprenticeships were not "the American way." He claimed that the apprentice system had been tried, but very few hotels would take students on an apprenticeship basis (Cornell Archives, 28/11/1803). This appears to be an instance of the feasibility of institutional solutions at one level being determined by institutions at a superordinate level (Holm 1995). The debate over an institutional structure for education in the hospitality industry takes place in the context of ideologies about education in American society. The role of taken-for-granted ideas of educational propriety in the evaluation of the apprenticeship alternative could be seen as an area of overlap between the conscious and preconscious schools of institutional theory.

The alternative of establishing in-house training programs was initially tried by some hotel chains. The Fred Harvey System had a training system dating back to the late nineteenth century. That system produced the Harvey Girl, the working version of the girl next door that became a part of American folklore (Moon 1980). United Hotels and Statler Hotels also attempted in-house training (Inman 1993). Interestingly, these early chains were the very organizations that fought hardest for a centralized training system. Their dissatisfaction with in-house training was probably because of the high mobility of labor among hospitality organizations[1]. Hotel employees traditionally stay in a job for a relatively short period before moving to another hotel (Uhrbrock 1930). Baum and Lant (1993) report that on average, managers in the Manhattan hotel industry have been with their current hotel for a little more than five years. If employees were likely to change employers frequently, then any hotel organization that incurred the cost of their training would end up paying to train another organization's workers. This system would provide a strong incentive for organizations that don't have their own training systems, but instead free-ride on the training efforts of others. The expectation would be that organizations with training systems would quickly grow dissatisfied under these conditions, and the historical evidence supports this.

With apprenticeship and in-house training being unacceptable, the challenge to the hotel industry was to implement the alternative of a centralized system. Two questions were critical for the centralized system: who would pay for it, and what type of training would be provided? Not surprisingly, hoteliers were united in their hope that the government would pay for education in the hospitality industry, but the issue of funding was important in the timing of efforts to establish centralized education, and in the choice of leaders for the project. In contrast, there was substantial disagreement among hoteliers regarding what type of training should be provided. Overwhelmingly, most hoteliers in the United States immediately after World War I operated small, independent hotels. These hoteliers wanted practical training at a level below college for clerks, wait-staff, and housekeepers. There were also a small number of hotel chain operators at this time. They favored university degree programs to produce professional managers. The process by which the hotel chain operators established their will is the story of institutionalization of education in this industry.

THE HISTORY OF THE EDUCATION PROJECT

The first efforts to revise education in the hospitality industry began two decades before the critical labor shortage that followed World War I. At the International Stewards Association (ISA) convention in 1903 there was a proposal to establish a Chair of Hotel Education at the Tuskegee Institute in Alabama (Hotel Monthly 1903). The same year, John Willy, editor of *Hotel Monthly*, began campaigning for technical schools for hotel workers. Willy expressed hope that "some philanthropist with the money of a Carnegie" would fund the schools, but if not, that "perhaps a society of hotel employers may be formed covering all America, to contribute, say, one-tenth of one percent of their payroll" (Willy 1903). A few years later Willy had changed his proposal a little, arguing for a national system backed by Federal and state governments (Willy 1905). In 1907, the ISA announced a more ambitious plan to build a hotel training school near Indianapolis. This plan was widely endorsed by hotel associations, but attempts to raise funds were unsuccessful (AHMA Archives, II 27).

Between 1911 and 1916 state hotel associations gave increasingly more attention to the labor problem, and members became convinced of Willy's position that the educational program should be handled at the national level (AHMA Archives, IV 68). One of the first suggestions that universities provide the education was made by John McFarlane Howie in 1907, and by 1911 there was some university participation in hotel education, with Columbia University and New York University offering courses in home economics and accounting that were promoted as being appropriate for hotel employees. Another alternative was provided by the Lewis Hotel Training School, which began in 1916. This private school, still in existence, began as a correspondence school and later established a residential school in Washington, D.C.

The noise about hospitality education reached a crescendo after World War I. The increased attention to the issue was partly prompted by the labor shortage of that period, but the issue of funding also affected the timing of the debate. Post-war retraining efforts made by the Federal government caught the attention of hoteliers. Specifically, the Smith-Hughes Act provided Federal funds for vocational training. There were a number of proposals for the hospitality industry to acquire a share of these funds by establishing high-school level training programs.

The contending proposals for hotel education were all presented at the AHA's 1920 meeting in Chicago. John McFarlane Howie was the chief advocate for hotel education at universities. His arguments centered on the economy of relying on universities rather than raising money to build schools dedicated to the hospitality industry, and on the ability of universities to provide the broad, liberal education that was suitable for a hotel executive. Howie's idea was supported by Professor Flora Rose, co-director (with Martha Van Rensselaer) of the School of Home Economics in the College of Agriculture at Cornell. Rose told the assembly that she thought Howie's proposal was quite reasonable, and that the correspondence between Howie and Cornell had been going on for more than five years. She also agreed with Howie on the importance of universities for helping hotel keeping obtain the status of a profession. A key difference between the university idea and the other alternatives for hotel education is that the other alternatives were all targeted at lower-level employees. H.J. Bohn (editor of *Hotel World*) responded to Howie by championing a lower-level technical school. Bohn had for many years tried to raise funds for the technical institute originally proposed by the ISA in 1907. Similarly, Gilbert Cowan, President of the American Caterers Association asked for help to establish a school for cooks and bakers. Edwin Piper, of the Lewis School, sought official recognition for that school, which unlike the alternatives, was already actively engaged in the business of hotel education (AHMA Archives, VI 4–8).

The response of the convention to the various proposals was indecisive. The resolution that was adopted cited the worsening labor situation, and the belief that Smith-Hughes funding of training in other industries was leading the "best young Americans" away from hotel careers. The approved proposition was to found a National Hotel Institute that would train both executives and lesser employees. The institute was also to serve as a clearing house for research in the hotel industry. To realize this vague vision, a committee of twenty-one was authorized to act on behalf of the AHA (AHMA Archives, VI 8–9).

The membership of the committee of twenty-one was a key determinant of the realization of the AHA's poorly defined proposal for an education institute. The committee included a disproportionate representation of hotel-chain entrepreneurs. Some of the committee members were the presidents of the largest hotel chains in the country such as John Bowman (Bowman Hotels), Lucious Boomer (Boomer-Dupont Properties), Frank Dudley (United Hotels), Eugene Eppley (Eppley Hotels), Ford Harvey (Fred Harvey Co.) and E.M. Statler (Statler Hotels). In fact, ten out of twenty hoteliers on the committee, including the chairman, were the heads of hotel chains (the twenty-first member was from the hotel press). This impressive representation of chain presidents occurred despite the fact that there were only 28 hotel chains in 1920, while there were more than 20,000 independently owned hotels. Adding to the influence of chain entrepreneurs, E.M.Tierney, an employee of John Bowman, soon replaced Bowman on the committee. In 1920 Tierney was AHA vice-president, and in 1921 he was elected president of the AHA.

Without officially disregarding alternatives, the education committee immediately concentrated its efforts on establishing a university degree program for hotel managers. Also from the beginning, most of the effort went to establishing this program at Cornell. The connection with Cornell grew out of a friendship that John McFarlane Howie had with Flora Rose and Martha Van Rensselaer of Cornell's Home Economics Department. Part of the attraction of Cornell was that by 1921 the Home Economics Department was offering some institutional management courses that seemed appropriate as building blocks for a hotel management program. Cornell may have also been favored due to the enthusiasm of administrators, particularly Rose. John Willy, who was influential from his position as editor of the *Hotel Monthly*, had some years earlier been converted to the university-education movement. He had raised the possibility of a hotel school in early 1920 at the University of Illinois, but found no interest from the head of the Home Economics Department there. Shortly after, Willy wrote to Cornell and received an enthusiastic reply from Rose, emphasizing the feasibility of a hotel school at Cornell (AHMA Archives, VI 6–7).

Frank Dudley, the head of United Hotels (at that time the largest chain in the country), led the negotiations with Cornell. Dudley was probably chosen for this role because he was a former New York State legislator and his Ten Eyck hotel in Albany was a political center. The original plan was to fund a Cornell hotel program with money from New York State. The intention of producing professional managers at Cornell was clear in Dudley's first communication with Cornell's acting president Albert W. Smith in a letter in January, 1920. In that letter Dudley asserted that "the hotel students at Cornell would be those destined for the highest levels of hotel management" (Cornell Archives). The June 1920 visit to Cornell of a seven member sub-committee of the committee of twenty-one represented the beginning of active negotiations. Five of the members of the sub-committee, including Dudley and Tierney, were chain entrepreneurs. A subsequent nine member education committee had six members who could be expected to favor the university education option, including Dudley as chairman, three chain entrepreneurs, John McFarlane Howie and John Willy (AHMA Archives, VI).

In negotiations, Dean Albert Mann of Cornell's School of Agriculture, within which the proposed hotel program would be operated, was most concerned that the money to operate the program should come from the State, or from the hotel industry. Mann also wanted to establish a curriculum that minimized the number of new courses, and courses outside the School of Agriculture, needed to satisfy hotel degree requirements. The curriculum was a key point for AHA representatives. This issue also demonstrates the particular interests of chain entrepreneurs in the type of education that would be provided. Chain entrepreneurs such as Lucious Boomer were adamant that the program should have a heavy emphasis on business courses such as accounting. The curriculum first proposed by Cornell had three credit hours of accounting. The one used when the program began in the fall of 1922 had nine credit hours of accounting, and six more hours were added in 1924 (Cornell Archives, 1/28/1803, 1–1). The interests of chain entrepreneurs were also furthered by the choice, at the recommendation of the AHA education committee, of Howard Meek to head the Cornell program. Meek disregarded the vision of home economists and liberal educators and instead worked to establish the completely specialized, practical curriculum favored by chain operators such as Boomer.

Even before the Cornell program accepted students, relationships with five hotel chains were established for training tours (Cornell Archives, 1/28/1803, 1–1). Chains also supported Cornell's program by paying for students to attend AHA annual meetings, lending executives to give lectures, and providing equipment (Cornell Archives, 1/28/1803). Ninety percent of the summer placements of the first class were with hotel chains. Illustrative of the relationship of Cornell's program to hotel chains is a 1924 letter from Professor Meek to United Hotels, stating that he "wanted particularly to let [United] have the pick of our class" (Cornell Archives, 1/28/1803, 1–3). A 1936 letter from Meek to W.I. Hamilton describes the careers of nine Cornell graduates, five of which were executives with hotel chains. Today, top executives of many hotel chains, including Holiday Inn, are graduates of Cornell's hotel school.

One effort where chain entrepreneurs and the whole hotel industry were frustrated was the attempt to obtain government financing for hotel education. Chain entrepreneurs, however, used their own resources when it became necessary. When alternatives for financing Cornell's hotel school failed, they contributed the necessary money themselves. Influential chain owners such as Dudley and Eppley gave $25,000 in 1922. Almost three decades later, E.M. Statler's will provided one million dollars to be used in "research work for the benefit of the hotel industry of the United States" (Cornell Archives, 28/1/1801, 5–14).

While the program at Cornell was being negotiated and started other universities were also considered for hotel programs. At the 1922 AHA meetings, Dudley explained that negotiations were "pending" with Harvard, Stanford, the University of Pennsylvania, and the Universities of Illinois, Iowa, and California (Cornell Archives, 1/28/1803, 1–1). In fact, a different cell of the AHA made a serious effort to establish a hotel school at the University of California's Berkeley campus at the same time the Cornell program was being established. Berkeley actually offered courses designed specifically for hotel students in the Fall of 1921, a whole year before Cornell, making it the first university to do so. The first major program established after Cornell was at Michigan State University. In 1994, there were more than 100 four-year degree programs in hospitality management.

COLLECTIVE ACTION TO CREATE INSTITUTIONS

To analyze the efforts of hotel chain entrepreneurs to change the institutions surrounding education, it is useful to think of the effort as collective action. Collective action is the term used to describe cooperative efforts to establish public goods. Public goods are assets that all members of a group have access to, regardless of their contributions to the action that provides the good. This feature of public goods is one of the things that makes collective action interesting. If members of the group will benefit regardless of contributions to collective action, we would expect them not to make contributions, instead free-riding on the efforts of others. If all members of the group analyze the situation the same way, as we would expect them to, then nobody will contribute to establish the public good. Education of managers is certainly a public good for the hospitality industry. The stock of managers is a resource upon which all organizations in the industry may draw. By considering why necessary resources were contributed despite the incentive to free-ride we can build a better understanding of the rise of hotel chains, and perhaps generate ideas that may be more generally applicable to understanding institutional change.

Financing for Hotel Schools

Money was one of the resources necessary to establish the programs that supplied the hotel industry with professional managers. The temptation for hotel organizations to free-ride on the efforts of others to establish hotel schools is clearly evident when we ask why an entrepreneur would contribute money to build such schools. There is no reasonable way that the graduates of a centralized training program can be restricted to be employed only by those who contributed to the establishment of the program. Hotel organizations would have the opportunity to hire university educated managers regardless of any financial contribution to establish the education program. So, it would seem rational for every hotel organization to withhold financial support for the education of managers, hoping to free-ride on the contributions of others.

One solution to this free-rider problem would be for a corporate body (such as the AHA) to coerce contributions from its members (Coleman 1990). This could be done, for example, by raising annual dues by ten dollars a year, and applying the added revenue to the education project. However, the AHA did not have the power to do this. Motions made at AHA annual meetings in favor of the education project were supported by the membership, but always with the stipulation that the AHA make no financial commitment (AHMA Archives). The problem was that the AHA had a heterogeneous membership, with rifts not only between chain hotels and independently owned hotels, but also between geographical regions. Its existence was tenuous enough that a demand that members support a university education project, especially one that was to start in the North East[2], would probably have destroyed the AHA.

Since coercion was not feasible, the champions of university hotel schools had to find other means of financing. There were a number of campaigns to raise the necessary monies. As early as 1906, a letter to the editor of the *Hotel Monthly* appealed to hoteliers to put up "a hundred dollars each toward establishing and maintaining a school for educating young men and women for hotel work" (Hotel Monthly 1906). In 1909 the International Stewards Association established a committee to raise the $250,000 necessary to establish a school of cookery and food service (AHMA Archives, II 27). In November 1921, Frank Dudley, then chairman of the AHA's education committee, launched "a historic education fund-raising campaign, the like of which the hotel world had never seen and may never see again" (AHMA Archives, VI 111).

Considering the free-rider problem, it is not surprising that these campaigns received warm public welcomes, and many promises of contributions, but ultimately very little actual money (AHMA Archives, II 27). Hoteliers all liked the idea of an educational program but wanted someone else to pay for it. The eventual solution to the financing problem reflected the fact that university hotel education programs promised to benefit the large hotel chains much more than other hotel organizations. In fact, the benefit to the large chains was potentially so large that it was apparently worth it to them to incur the whole cost of establishing the Cornell program. When efforts to raise money from the general hotel community and from government sources failed, the chains had a simple choice: to finance the program themselves (and allow smaller organizations to free-ride) or to give up the idea of university education for hotel managers. They chose the former. The significant contributions to the education fund were made by John Bowman, Lucious Boomer, Eugene Eppley, E.M. Statler and Frank Dudley; each the president of a large hotel chain (Cornell Archives, 28/1/1803, 1–44).

Acquiring the Sanction of Independent Hoteliers

A second necessary resource for university hotel schools or any other alternative for centralized hotel education was the sanction of the AHA. The supply of this resource is particularly interesting because independent hoteliers, who made up most of the AHA when education was being debated, favored lower-level alternatives to universities, such as technical and cooking schools. So, the problem is not simply how independent hoteliers were convinced to give their sanction to university hotel schools rather than free-ride, but rather how chain entrepreneurs were able to overcome the strong interest independent hoteliers had in alternative institutional arrangements.

Chain entrepreneurs had some very practical organizational advantages in the institutional contest with independent hoteliers. The consistent over-representation of chain entrepreneurs on the education committees of the AHA appears to have been instrumental in the establishment of university hotel schools. One reason for this over-representation may have been that chain entrepreneurs had more freedom to participate in political and professional affairs than did the proprietors of independent hotels (AHMA Archives). It may also be that it was easier for the smaller group of chain operators to recognize and act upon their shared interest in professional education. As DiMaggio (1988) has argued, institutional change often requires coalitions of actors, and it is surely easier to manage a coalition of 28 actors (the number of hotel chains in 1921) than 20,000 (the number of independent hotels). Further, although independent hotels shared the need for lower-level employees, they were heterogenous in a number of other dimensions. They had different geographic locations which affected what they wanted from an education program. Also they differed on dimensions such as the size, age, and quality of their hotels. These differences may have inhibited their ability to cooperate to establish education for lower-level employees.

Chain entrepreneurs have also benefited from the ability to appeal to the higher motives of hoteliers. Building coalitions is facilitated by the ability of actors to present their interests as altruistic, and by the consistency of proposed institutions with basic values in society. An important reason for both of these coalition-building advantages is that they increase the likelihood of finding actors who share interests (Ingram, 1997). Additionally, institutional entrepreneurs that champion altruistic interests and interests consistent with societal values have rhetoric advantages. Alexander and Smith (1993) suggests that there is a discursive structure of civil society, a democratic (and counter-democratic) code that can be used to legitimate political activity, although in an important difference from the argument here, they do not see the classifications of actors and actions according to such discourse as subject to debate and strategic maneuvering. An example of the role of consistency of institutional claims with society's basic values in the hotel education debate is the fate of the apprenticeship alternative. Apprenticeship appears to have been inconsistent with the basic values that were active in the United States after World War I and this appears to have hurt the evaluation of what seems like a feasible alternative. Further, the enemies of apprenticeship clearly had a rhetoric advantage, as evidenced by Meek's claim that apprenticeship was "un-American."

Perhaps most important to hotel education, however, was the possibility of framing university programs in an altruistic way. One of the most effective strategies that chain operators used was to emphasize the ability of a university education program to confer professional status on hoteliers. For example, during the 1920 debate that resulted in the establishment of the committee of twenty-one, Howie responded to a claim that universities could not train the dishwashers and waiters that hotels required by explaining that universities produced lawyers and engineers, not their menial employees. By arguing that professional status was the purpose of the university education program, chain operators could seem unselfish and in support of the interests of all hoteliers. Status was a widely shared interest around which it was possible to rally the diverse actors in this industry.

Evidence of the growing importance to hoteliers of professional status was the election in 1921 of E.M. Tierney to the AHA Presidency: "Coming to the AHA Presidency just when hotelmen began to dream of college degrees as a means of lifting their occupation to professional status, Tierney's supporters could recall dozens of his well publicized speeches in which he begged hotelmen to think and act as proud professional men, and he was reportedly the first college graduate to preside over that organization" (AHMA Archives, VI 83). Tierney recognized that the university education program was the surest means of raising the status of hoteliers. He gave Frank Dudley great power to establish the education program by putting him in charge of the nine member education committee, recognizing that this appointment might be the most important decision of his administration (AHMA Archives, IV 93).

The independent hotelier who was most active in establishing the Cornell hotel school was also an excellent example of the dreams of independent hoteliers regarding the possibility of professional status, and ironically, the most embittered by the ultimate form of the Cornell Hotel School. John McFarlane Howie disagreed passionately with Lucious Boomer and other chain entrepreneurs on what Cornell's curriculum should be. Howie (himself capable of quoting Shakespeare "by the yard") favored a liberal-arts curriculum for the hotel students. He felt they should be educated to increase their elegance (and presumably the status of all hoteliers) rather than to increase their business acumen. Years later, Howie was extremely bitter about what the Cornell hotel school had become at the hands of the chain entrepreneurs. In 1945, shortly before his death, he observed that "it is sad that a great educational institution can prostitute itself for a million dollars" (Cornell Archives, 28/1/1803, 1–46).

There were of course other factors that helped the chain entrepreneurs establish the institutional framework that favored themselves. Perhaps most important was the fact that they were richer than other actors. The relevance of this is clearly demonstrated by the large financial contributions chain entrepreneurs made to found the Cornell Hotel School. Chain entrepreneurs also had social networks that increased their power (Granovetter 1991). Frank Dudley was a former state legislator in New York, and the perception that this increased his ability to obtain state funding for the Cornell project was one reason he was given authority. Chains also helped directly in the education of professional managers for the hotel industry by providing educational resources. For example, in 1937, F.A. McKowne, then President of Statler Hotels, was able to convince National Cash Register to donate to Cornell equipment for use in teaching accounting to hotel students.

Institutional Change Hypotheses

The changes in the institutional environment that chain entrepreneurs caused should contribute to the success of hotel chains. Chains require professional managers, and hotel schools such as Cornell are a demonstrated excellent source of these managers. When professional managers are available to the hotel industry, as they were in increasing numbers since 1922, hotel chains will have an easier time filling the managerial positions that are critical to the success of chains. Greater numbers of professional managers will make it easier to found hotel chains, and once the chains are in existence, easier for them to survive.

Hypothesis 3: The mortality risk of hotel chains will decrease as the supply of professional managers increases.

Hypothesis 4: The founding rate of hotel chains will increase as the supply of professional managers increases.

5

Technological Change: The Development of Internal Control

Problems of managerial control (hereafter called agency problems) inhibited the growth of hotel chains. The development of accounting and managerial information solutions to these problems was an important step in the transition to professional management in the hotel industry. Without the technology of internal control, personal supervision was the only way the owners of a hotel could be certain that employees were working hard and acting honestly. Internal control systems made it possible for owners to lead increasingly large organizations and be confident of the fidelity of their employees. Before detailing this argument and the historical support for it, I will describe agency problems in general and their manifestation in the hotel industry.

AGENCY PROBLEMS

The owners of an organization have a claim to the residual earnings after paying all expenses. Their interests are best served if the organization maximizes profit. However, in professionally managed organizations it is not the owners, but the employees who are responsible for maximizing profit. As Jensen and Meckling (1976, 308) observe, if both the owner and the manager are utility maximizers, "there is good reason to believe that the [employee] will not always act in the best interests of the [owner]." Jensen and Meckling define an agency relationship as a contract under which one or more persons (the principal(s)) engage another person (the agent) to perform some service on their behalf which involves delegating some decision making authority to the agent. They define agency costs as the sum of (1) the monitoring expenditures by the principal; (2) the bonding expenditures by the agent; and (3) the reduction in the principal's welfare due to failure by the agent to maximize the principal's welfare, referred to as the residual loss.

In service organizations such as hotels the agency problem can be particularly severe. Because there are no physical materials that are transacted it can be easy for employees to steal from the owners. For instance, a fraud involving the foreign exchange account of a hotel does not leave the physical trace that makes employee theft from a manufacturer easier to detect. Geller (1991, 5) lists other reasons that make the hotel industry more vulnerable to employee theft and embezzlement:

- many cash transactions
- small business units (even within large chains)
- jobs with low social status
- items having relatively high value (e.g., wine and steaks)
- inventories of commodities employees also use

Traditional Solution to Agency Problems

The agency problems described above affect not only hotel chains, but also the organizational form they replaced, the independent hotel. However, independent hotels did not have to rely on accounting controls to solve agency problems. Often such hotels employed family members of the owner. In any case, the owner was both intimately familiar with the operation of the hotel, and closer to the employees. Close proximity between owner and employee allows direct supervision more effective than that which is possible in a large hierarchy. As Frank (1988) notes, there are subtle biological signals of malfeasance. If an employee is dishonest, a resident owner will be more likely to perceive such signals, and more likely to actually observe evidence of malfeasance. But there is a more important way that close proximity between owner and employee discourages employee malfeasance. Such closeness creates personal relationships which are an important mechanism for maintaining social order.

Granovetter (1985) argues that concrete personal relations and networks of such relations are vital in discouraging malfeasance. He observes that "continuing economic relations often become overlaid with social content that carries strong expectations of trust and abstention from opportunism" (490). Certainly personal relationships establish repeated interactions, which can encourage cooperation between self-interested actors, but Granovetter's position goes further. It attributes a special character to personal relationships. They create trust, which is more than the concurrence of rational interests.

So independent hotels could rely on personal supervision and personal relationships to minimize employee malfeasance. But for larger organizations these mechanisms are not available. The owner of a hotel chain cannot spend as much time in any single hotel. Supervisors can be hired, but they do not have the same incentive to monitor employees that the owner does. These problems are worse if the chain is owned by many investors. Not only will personal relationships between owners and employees be missing but the employees may have trouble even visualizing the owners. Whatever role conscience plays in controlling employee dishonesty will be at a minimum when it is some faceless corporate entity that is being cheated.

Internal Control Solutions to Agency Problems

A different solution to agency problems was required to enable large professionally managed organizations to develop in the hotel industry. The solution that developed in this and other industries was internal control as part of an accounting system. Before 1910 the typical hotel had nothing that resembled a modern accounting system. As one observer put it, "there is no other business that is run so unsystematically and with so little regard to the first principles of business as the average country hotel" (Clarenbach 1907, 18). Many hotels were unable to determine if they were profitable or unprofitable (AHMA Archives). Starting around 1910 hotel accounting, and its internal control mechanisms, became increasingly sophisticated. Before describing these systems, and the causes of their development, I will illustrate their role in prohibiting employee malfeasance.

A traditional form of fraud in hotels is for the front-desk clerk to not record the arrival of a guest in the hotel's bookkeeping system and when the guest pays, to simply pocket the payment. Since the guest doesn't use anything that can be counted by staying at the hotel, there is no easy way for the hotel's ownership to recognize a fraud of this type because to the ownership there is no evidence that there ever was a guest. Even if the guest had made a reservation, the clerk could say that the guest had called to cancel it. Hotel registers, which guests sign upon arrival, may exist partly to prevent this fraud, but registers provide a very limited control because it is not difficult to cause the guest not to sign the register, for instance by hiding it.

A control that prevents this fraud is described in the *Hotel Monthly* in 1902. The control, called in that article "Saiter's duplicate room chart sheets" consists of two charts listing all the rooms of the hotel. One chart is kept by the front-desk clerk, who checks every room that is occupied. A second chart is kept by the housekeeper, who checks every room that is unoccupied. Every day, the hotel owner, or a senior manager can compare the two lists. If the front-desk list shows a room as unoccupied when the housekeeper's list shows the room as occupied there is evidence that the front-desk clerk may be defrauding the hotel. This control is not perfect. It could be overcome by collusion between the housekeeper and the front-desk clerk, but such collusion is difficult to sustain for an extended period of time. It is generally accepted that if an internal control system prevents fraud in the absence of collusion, it is a good system. The system would provide even better control if the housekeeper had an incentive to correctly fill out the room chart. A simple way to provide this incentive would be to make the housekeeper's pay contingent on the number of rooms occupied and therefore in need of cleaning. The practice of generating and comparing lists of rooms occupied from the front desk and the housekeeping department is still used in hotels.

THE DEVELOPMENT OF HOTEL ACCOUNTING AND INTERNAL CONTROL

Because large organizations require internal controls, it is not surprising that the first comprehensive hotel accounting systems were created by the earliest hotel chains (Ingram 1996). In fact, the first hotel chain, the Fred Harvey System, developed an accounting system so innovative that it was a major influence on the industry. Other early chains such as the Flagler hotels in Florida, the Statler hotels and Frank Dudley's United Hotels chain were also instrumental in leading the accounting revolution in the hotel industry (AHMA Archives, IV 81, VI 25). The Boss hotel chain had a control system that was viewed as instrumental to the success of the chain (Hotel Monthly 1939). The chains even contributed to mechanical advances in control. National Cash Register credited E.M. Statler with advising in the development of its front office posting machine (Cornell Archives, 28/1/1803, 1–6).

Another impetus for the development of accounting systems in the hotel industry was to allow a response to many legislative threats. Starting with prohibition, there were a number of public movements that pressured hotels to demonstrate their costs and profitability. There were also occasional drives for government regulation of room rates. In 1920 the industry found itself "under constant fire from an irate public which demanded drastic reductions in both room rates and restaurant prices . . . The traveling salesmen's associations, backed by numerous newspapers, were loudly demanding that a federal commission be established to regulate hotel rates, arguing that hotels were public utilities necessary to interstate commerce. Some insisted that the projected commission outlaw tipping as well" (AHMA Archives, VI 18). The only response hotels could make to threats such as these was to demonstrate that they were not making monopoly profits. This required accounting procedures that were comparable across hotels, creating an external need supplementary to the internal need of control.

The Diffusion of Accounting and Control Systems

Three groups were primarily responsible for the diffusion of accounting and internal control systems in the hotel industry (Ingram 1996). Trade associations represented the whole industry, and were particularly concerned with responses to political threats. Hotel chains developed internal controls for their own purposes, but diffused them in efforts to train managers. Public accounting firms were in an ideal position to collect the best elements of their clients' systems and integrate them into packages to offer back to clients.

The most important contribution of national and regional trade associations was the development and publication of the *Uniform System of Accounts*, first published in 1926 by the New York City Hotel Association. This volume detailed a classification system for the transactions of a hotel. Hotels using this system could use comparative analysis for management purposes. By consistently assigning expenses and revenues to the same accounts, ratios can be calculated, and changes in costs can be quickly identified. Further, with many hotels using the same accounts it became possible to create the type of industry-wide statistics that were necessary to lobby on behalf of the industry.

The early chains assisted in the diffusion of internal control technology in two ways. First, they trained their personnel in their systems, and these personnel often went to other organizations, taking accounting expertise with them. It was not uncommon for a hotel to advertise that its management had been "Statler trained" (e.g., Hotel Red Book 1926, 124). Second, the early hotel chains insisted on inclusion of accounting as part of the training that universities offered for hotel managers. The United Hotel Chain even released its auditors' reports for use in teaching accounting at Cornell (AHMA Archives, VI 50).

The two dominant public accounting firms in the industry were Horwath and Horwath, founded in 1915 and Harris, Kerr, Forster and Company, founded in 1907. These firms were in a position to investigate and analyze the accounting and control systems of their clients. This allowed them to identify the most effective procedures and integrate them in systems which they offered back to their clients. Members of these firms, particularly Horwath and Horwath, were also instrumental in the accounting training of new hotel managers. Horwath and Toth of that firm wrote the first text on hotel accounting (1928). Further, members of Horwath and Horwath taught hotel accounting courses at New York University, Cornell, DePaul University, the University of Southern California and Michigan State University in the 1920s (The Horwath Hotel Accountant 1930).

An illustration of the role of accounting firms in diffusing controls is given by the "How they got away with it" feature of Horwath and Horwath's monthly magazine for employees, *Alarm Clock*, which began publication in 1921. This feature described true incidents of hotel fraud and discussed preventative internal controls. For example, one month the article addressed a fraud where the front-desk clerk entered an amount in the hotel's books that was smaller than the amount the customer paid and kept the difference (Alarm Clock 1928, 5). The fraud events were discovered in Horwath and Horwath's audits and therefore were based on the experience of the hospitality industry. With the information from the articles, Horwath and Horwath's employees could implement tighter internal control systems for other clients.

The Controls Themselves

The internal controls that developed can be divided into two classes, procedures and mechanical controls (Ingram 1996). The procedures were centered around the observance of a number of basic principles of internal control. Geller (1991) describes some of these principles as maintaining a division of duties, fixing responsibilities on one individual, limiting access to assets, requiring vacations and rotating employees, and scheduling frequent external audits. Well defined roles, practices, forms for recording information, and independent checks of transactions became increasingly more common in the hotel industry. Examples of effective internal control practices include the practice discussed earlier of having maids fill out reports on the occupancy of the rooms; using pre-numbered forms for billing; having different employees responsible for handling cash and recording and verifying transactions; and rotating key employees among positions or even hotels. An indication of the volume of potential control practices for hotels is the seven-page questionnaire with more than 200 questions that Pannell, Kerr, Forster uses to evaluate the internal control environment in the hotels it audits.

The earliest mechanical advances were designed to prevent frauds where the amount entered into the hotel's books is less than the amount charged to the customer by insuring that the two amounts were identical. The original methods of doing this used carbons and layered forms to copy the same entry in multiple places such as the hotel's receipt register and the customer's bill. The next great advance was the cash register, offering multiple and even secret totals that could not be turned back by employees. In 1948 National Cash Register introduced a bookkeeping machine for hotel front offices, which according to Podd (1950, 24) "provides as good a control as any mechanical device can." According to a 1948 advertisement this machine provided "guests' bills, account cards, journal sheets, and posting vouchers with machine-printed verification of posting on each voucher . . . in one simultaneous operation. All figures must be in absolute agreement."

The introduction of the computer represented a great advance for mechanized control systems in hotels. As early as 1950 at least one hotel was using a punch-card method to control beverage costs (Podd, 1950). In 1966 Cornell's hotel school published a research study called *A New Hotel Management System Based upon Data Processing in a Computer Center* (Sayles and MacLennan 1966). The system described provided for reservations, registration, payroll, and cost control for food and beverage. Of course, as computers became more powerful their role in hotel accounting and internal control increased. Now computers manage extremely sophisticated systems of reservations, registration, billing and cost control. The Hyatt chain is even experimenting with a system that allows guests to use their credit card as a room key, bypassing the registration desk all together.

The role of procedures and mechanical controls can be further illustrated by considering the application of both sources of control to the common problem of controlling the flow of alcohol in the hotel bar. The bar is traditionally an area of control weakness because of the difficulty of closely monitoring the inventory of alcohol during a shift, and because of the many cash transactions. If the bartender gives away drinks, or pockets cash, the hotel can suffer significant losses. A procedural solution to this problem used by the Warden hotel chain is to charge the bartender for the alcohol used at retail prices (Hotel Monthly 1912). With this procedure, it is the bartender that loses if the hotel does not receive full retail price for the alcohol consumed by customers. A mechanical control for the bar that has developed much more recently is to have automatic drink dispensers, which dispense alcohol in exact amounts and keep an accurate total of how many drinks were served during a shift. Mechanical controls such as this sometimes inhibit efficient operations of the hotel, for instance by slowing down bar service, but the number of mechanical controls that offer hotels a profitable trade-off of control for efficiency is constantly increasing. The understanding of control in service organizations would benefit from more research on the relationship between control and efficiency.

Technological Change Hypotheses

The progressive development of control systems used in the hospitality industry reduces agency costs. As controls improve, hotels within a chain are less likely to suffer losses from employee fraud and managers within the chain will have more information that is useful for analyzing operations and motivating employees. These benefits of control systems should make it more attractive to found hotel chains, and more likely that they will survive once founded.

Hypothesis 5: The mortality rate of hotel chains will decrease as agency costs fall.

Hypothesis 6: The founding rate of hotel chains will increase as agency costs fall.

To conclude this chapter I'll provide an illustration of the combined effect of all of the internal control advances described. Podd (1950, 23) claims:

> A convincing proof of the great development of internal control in hotels is afforded by a comparison of the rate which surety companies charged for bonding hotel employees 25 years ago and the rate they charge today. The basic rate for bonding hotel employees 25 years ago was just about twice as high per thousand dollars of bond as the rate for department store cashiers and bank tellers. But in the past 25 years the bonding rate for hotel employees has been reduced by 25%, and today the rate is the same as that for department store cashiers and about 30% lower than the

> rate for bank tellers. In other words, while in the first quarter of the century the slipshod accounting methods of hotels made hotel cashiers and bookkeepers bad risks for surety companies, today hotel bookkeepers and cashiers are considered among the best risks.

The bonding he describes is fidelity bonding, an insurance against employee dishonesty. Figure 5–1 shows fidelity bonding rates (CPI adjusted) for the hotel industry from 1896 to 1980. Except for the depression, these rates are constantly decreasing. This demonstrates that actuaries determined that the risk of employee malfeasance in the hotel industry decreased greatly during the twentieth century.

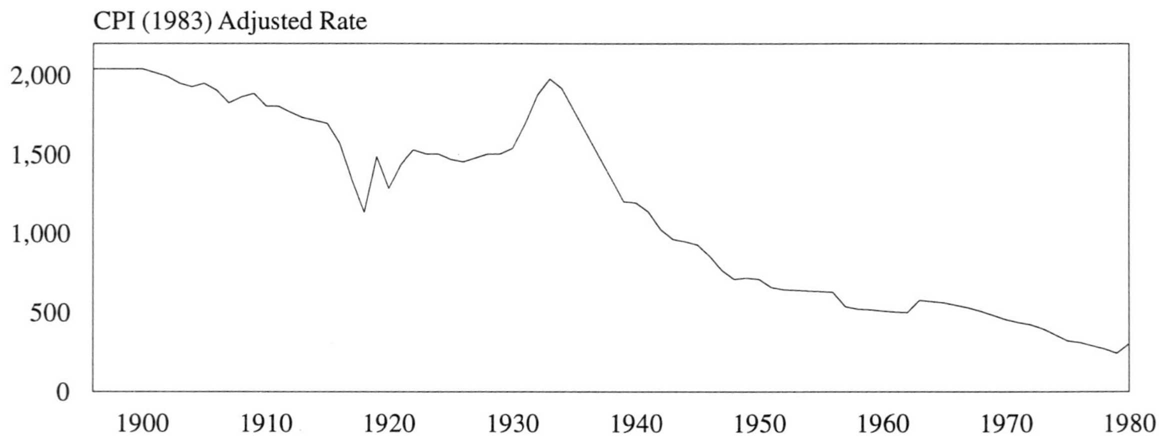

Figure 5-1. Fidelity Bonding Rates.
Rates for $100,000 blanket bond, 100 employees.
Source: Surety Association of America

6

Methodological Overview and Data

This chapter provides an overview of the methodological approach used to examine the rise of hotel chains, and describe the collection of data and the variables used. The three chapters that follow discuss in detail the methods used and present results of statistical analyses.

ANALYTIC STRATEGY

There are three ways that hotel chains, or any other type of organization can become more or less prominent. Their mortality rate can decrease or increase; their founding rate can increase or decrease; and existing chains can grow or shrink. Changes in mortality and founding rates cause changes in the number of chains. Changes in the size of existing chains change the "mass" of the population without changing its numbers. All three of these determinants of the prominence of a population will be studied here. Brief descriptions of the methods are given below.

Mortality Processes

Mortality processes are investigated by estimating the instantaneous risk (the hazard) of death of chains. The unit of analysis is the individual chain, so chain level as well as environmental variables can be studied. Features of a chain that may make it more robust than another chain, such as the strategy for naming units, are modeled. Features of the environment that may make the chains that exist at any given time more robust than chains that exist at other times, such as the number of professional managers, are also modeled. The data used has an observation for every year in the life of every hotel chain that I was able to find. Hypotheses 1a, 1b, 2, 3, and 5 are tested.

Founding Processes

For founding processes, the individual chain is not a feasible unit of analysis. It is impossible to define the risk set of social actors that may form a hotel chain. Therefore, the unit of analysis is the population (Hannan and Freeman 1989). There are two options for analyzing the rate at which foundings occur in a population. If the time of the foundings is known with precision, hazard models can be used to estimate the "risk" of a founding occurring at any moment (for example, see Hannan and Freeman 1987 on labor union founding). When the exact time of foundings is not known, the number of foundings in a discrete period may be analyzed with event count models (for example, see Hannan and Freeman 1989 on semiconductor producer founding). The available data for hotel chains only provides the year in which chains were founded, not the exact date of chain founding, so I use the second option and analyze the number of foundings in each year. Because the unit of analysis is the population, chain-level variables cannot be modeled. So, the arguments about strategic features of chains (chapter 3) cannot be tested. However, hypothesis 4 and hypothesis 6 about the effect of environmental manipulations are tested in the founding analysis.

Dynamics of Size

The dynamics of organizational growth and decline are not as well understood as mortality or founding. For this reason, I have not offered hypotheses about changes in chain size. However, size must be analyzed because the full effect of the influences I discuss should be recognized. Further, there are not established methods for studying organizational size as a dependent variable. Following Freeman and Hannan (1975), I use partial-adjustment models to study changes in chain size. These dynamic models allow me to investigate the causes of growth and decline of hotel chains. Because the unit of analysis is the individual chain, the analysis includes both chain-level and population-level effects.

DATA

The data represent the population of hotel chains in the U.S. from 1896 to 1980. The date of the beginning of observation was because 1896 was the earliest time for which I could find a source of data. There is some evidence that hoteliers shared ownership of hotels prior to the civil war, but the earliest hotel chain I could find was the Fred Harvey System, founded in 1878. Since some chains predated 1896, it is necessary to consider the possibility of a left-censoring problem. If chains existed before 1896, then the ones I find in 1896 may be atypical in unseen ways; they have survived, while other chains (presumably less "fit") may have been founded and died without observation. However, there were only three chains in existence in 1896, and two of those die by 1896 (the other is the Fred Harvey System). Therefore, 1896 is close enough to the beginning of the population of hotel chains that left censoring is not a problem.

1980 was chosen for the end of observation because of both practical and theoretical reasons. In 1980 the population of hotel chains is large, and it grows larger in the subsequent decade. That decade also sees a notable increase in activity that leads to the mortality and founding of chains. In fact, it became necessary for the directory that lists hotel chains to begin publishing multiple addendum between editions to keep up with re-organizational activity. This makes collecting data on the population past 1980 extremely laborious. I speculate that the period 1980–1990 would have taken as long as the period 1896–1980 to code and input, and therefore would have added one year to the time necessary to complete this study. However, more important than the cost of extending the observation period is the fact that data after 1980 may be inappropriate for studying the processes of interest here. The growth and dynamic activity of hotel chains since 1980 has been attributed to causes that are unique to that period. For example, many in the industry blame the faulty analysis of a single consulting firm for industry-wide over-building in that period. Also, hotel chains were caught in the furor of acquisition and divestment that affected many organizations in the 1980s. These atypical (and largely unoperationalizable) features of the post-1980 environment of hotel chains led me to decide to stop observation at 1980.

Hotel chains are defined as any organization that operates three or more hotels or motels. In the analyses I control for whether the chain consisted predominantly of hotels or motels. I also control for (or investigated in unreported models) the effects of various ownership structures that resulted in the operation of the hotels. For instance, I control for the number of hotels that are franchised from another organization, and I tested for effects of leasing hotels from others. The level of three hotels was chosen because of my interest in hotel chains as professionally managed organizations. Two hotels may be operated in the traditional manner, especially if they are close to each other. But with three hotels, the proprietor is significantly less able to have a physical presence at each location, and management is necessary.

Further, the AHMA defines a hotel chain as operating three units, so their directories can be used for data collection.

Sources of Data and Method of Collection

The two main sources of data were:

- the *Directory of Hotel Systems*, published annually since 1931 by the AHMA. This directory claims to include every hotel chain in the U.S., and gives the location of units; and
- the *Hotel Redbook*, published annually since 1896 (by the AHMA since the late 1920s). This is the most extensive directory of individual hotels. However, its coverage is not complete. It lists hotels by location, and provides some information about ownership.

In addition, archives kept by the AHMA, and industry journals were used. For the period before 1931, chains were identified by scanning the *Hotel Redbook* for advertisements of chains. Also, every fifth year the complete directory was scanned to identify units with common ownership that were not advertised as chains. Once a chain was identified, its units could be traced to previous editions of the Redbook to find the year of its founding. For years after 1930, the *Directory of Hotel Systems* was the principal source of information. However, for every founding or death, the Redbook was consulted to verify the year in which the event happened. Further, the ownership of every unit in the chain was found in the *Redbook* to determine the conditions of founding or death (e.g., was the chain absorbed partially by another?).

Using this procedure I documented the event histories of 989 hotel chains. These event histories comprised 9685 one-year spells. Although it was my goal to find every hotel chain that existed in the period of study, it is likely that some were missed. However, in my reading of historical documents relating to this industry I have not found evidence of a single chain that is not in my data. In fact, I documented many chains that industry historians were unaware of. Therefore, I conclude that my data includes nearly all of the hotel chains that existed between 1896 and 1980.

Table 6–1 shows basic statistics for the population-level variables used in the analyses. Statistics for these variables are given both by chain spell and by population year. The difference in the means of these two presentations is because there are unequal numbers of chains in any year.

Table 6–1
Basic Statistics: Population-Level Variables
Hotel Chains, 1896–1980

Variable	Mean	By Spell S.D.	Min	Max	Obs	By Year (85 observations) Mean	S.D.
Log(Professional Managers)	4.081	1.68	-2.3	5.44	9685	1.96	3.17
Agency Cost	75.47	46.7	24.32	204.02	9685	116.6	60.4
Density	175.2	67.2	3	308	9685	112.52	84.0
$Density^2$	35220	24006	9	94864	9685	20305	23244
Occupancy	69.2	9.74	51	93	9685	69.0	8.2
Independent Hotels (1000's)	61.45	21.04	28.27	84.5	9685	47.67	22.4
Aggregate Chain Units	3068	2731	13	8862	9685	1658.8	2236.2
Aggregate Franchise Units	206.7	363.8	0	1110	9685	86.89	249

Table 6–2
Basic Statistics: Chain-Level Variables
Hotel Chains, 1896–1980

Variable	Mean	S.D.	Min	Max	Obs
Log(Hotels)	1.855	0.91	0.693	7.414	9606
Name Concentration	0.404	0.30	0	1	9606
City Concentration	0.466	0.32	0	1	9606
Regions	2.105	1.77	1	9	9685
Log(Age)	1.56	1.64	-2.3	4.625	9685
Motel	0.15	0.35	0	1	9683
Franchisor	0.026	0.16	0	1	9685
Referral System	0.012	0.11	0	1	9685
National Park	0.03	0.19	0	1	9685
Log(Foreign Hotels)	-2.04	0.99	-2.3	6.75	9606
Hotels Franchised	0.768	3.6	0	76	9614

The spell mean is the year values weighted by the number of chains alive during each year. Table 6–2 shows basic statistics for chain-level variables. Descriptions of each variable follow.

Population-Level Variables

Log(Professional Managers). This variable represents the supply of professional managers available to hotel chains in any year. Optimally, I would have the total number of educated managers in the hospitality industry. That data is not available. There are statistics kept of university degrees granted, but hotel management degrees were not broken out from general business degrees in these statistics until the 1970s. Instead, I rely on the number of graduates from Cornell's hotel management program. The central role this program played in hotel education makes it a suitable proxy for the growth of professional management in the industry. Numbers of graduates were obtained from the *Registrar's Report*, 1896–1980. The log (all logs mentioned in this study are natural logs) is used to reflect the fact that the sophistication of managers in the industry probably increases at a decreasing rate with the number of graduates.

The operationalization of the supply of professional managers is by necessity a proxy. So, it is necessary to consider other proxies that may more closely represent the supply of professional managers. One alternative is to use the stock of Cornell Hotel School graduates rather than the flow. The log of total living Cornell Hotel School graduates was used in alternative estimations of models in chapters 7 and 8.

Agency Cost. The historic risk of employee malfeasance in an industry is particularly difficult to operationalize. The first option I considered was to produce some scale of the sophistication of the control systems that I argue addressed the agency problem for hotel chains. There are two challenges to doing this. First, it would be necessary to document all of the control system innovations in the hospitality industry during the last century, and to estimate the rate and extent of their diffusion. Second, the effects of the innovations must somehow be quantified. I can imagine (if not actually obtain) information that would allow me to solve the first problem. However, quantifying the effects of these innovations across an industry, dating back a century, is probably impossible.

The operationalization I use here, fidelity bonding rates, has the advantages of being relatively easy to obtain, and of having a compelling connection to agency cost. Fidelity bonding is a type of insurance employers can take out against the risk of employee malfeasance, and is commonly used in the hospitality industry (Geller 1991). It is insurance against the agency problem. Rates vary for individual organizations due to past claims, but base rates vary by industry. I obtained information from the Surety Association that allowed me to calculate the basic rate (for a typical level of bond) over the observation period. The Surety Association is the organization that recommends base rates to insurance companies. The time series I used in the analysis is shown in Figure 5–1. Bond costs were corrected for inflation using the Consumer Price Index, and divided by 10 in the analyses.

Density and *Density*^{2}. Density is the number of hotel chains that exist at the beginning of the year of observation.

Occupancy Rate. The occupancy rate is the percentage of hotel-room nights that were sold in the U.S. in a given year. Rates were obtained from Horwath and Horwath (1968) and directly from the AHMA.

Independent Hotels. This is the number of hotels that are independently owned (i.e., not part of a chain). Data were taken from the census of services. Census reports are published about every five years. The variable is the number of independent hotels shown in the last census report before the observation.

Aggregate Chain Units. This is the total number of hotels that are part of all chains. Aggregate chain units and independent hotels should add to the total number of hotels in the U.S.

Aggregate Franchise Units. This is the number of chain units that are franchises. It is the total of the chain-level variable "Hotels Franchised". Independently owned hotels that are franchised are not included in this number, so it understates the actual total franchise units by some unknown amount. There is no way to determine how many independent franchise units there were in any year.

Chain-Level Variables

Log(Hotels). This is the number of hotels or motels in the chain. It represents the size of the chain. Freeman, Carroll and Hannan (1983) argue that the effect of size on organizational mortality decreases as the organization grows, so the log is used. An alternative measure of size is the number of rooms in the chain. That measure is preferable to units because a chain may consist of units that are smaller or larger (in terms of rooms) than the average. I collected data on rooms for most of the chains in the study. However, room counts are unavailable for a large block of observations, from 1930 to the mid-1950s. Because of the bias that eliminating all of those observations would produce, room counts cannot be used to measure size.

Name Concentration. This is the percentage of units in a chain that have the most dominant name used by the chain. To be counted as sharing a name it is not necessary that two units have exactly the same name. They must only share some identifiable term that links them. For example, here are the names of Doral Hotels Corporation units in 1978:

Doral Country Club	Miami, FL
Carillon Hotel	Miami Beach, FL
Doral Beach Hotel	Miami Beach, FL
Doral Inn	New York, NY
Doral Park Avenue Hotel	New York, NY
Tuscany Hotel	New York, NY
Tuscany Tower	New York, NY

There are two identifiable terms that link units: Doral and Tuscany. Four units are associated with Doral and two are associated with Tuscany. Therefore, Doral is the dominant name and is used to calculate Name Concentration. There are 7 units, and 4 have the name Doral, so the Name Concentration is 4/7 = .57. For chains where no two units share a name the Name Concentration is 1 / number of units.

When chains were founded, I traced the units in the chain to their existence before the chain to determine if the new chain's Name Concentration was a function of whether it had purchased or built its units. For instance, it might be that chains do not change the names of the units they acquire but give the units they build common names. If this were true, a low Name Concentration would occur when the new chain purchases units, and a high Name Concentration would occur when the new chain builds units. Tracing the units that originally composed the chain, however, did not reveal any relationship between whether the units were purchased or built, and the initial Name Concentration of the chain.

City Concentration. This is the percentage of units in a chain that exist in the city where the chain is best represented. For example, Doral Hotel Corporation units are in two cities: Miami and New York (close geographic areas that could reasonably be classified as part of the same city, like Miami and Miami Beach, were treated as the same city to calculate City Concentration). There are three units in Miami and four in New York, so the chain is best represented in New York. The City Concentration is 4/7 = .57. If the chain did not have two units in any one city, the City Concentration would be 1 / number of units.

Regions. Regions is the number of census regions in which the chain operated. There are a total of nine regions covering the fifty states (for example, the Western region includes Hawaii, California, Oregon, Washington and Alaska). If the chain had at least one unit in a region it was counted as operating in that region.

Log(Age). Age is the year of the observation minus the year the chain first appeared. In the first year of its existence, age is treated as .1 so the log can be calculated. If a chain dies and is reborn (for instance if it operated three hotels, fell to two and ceased to be a chain, then added one and became a chain again), its age during its "second life" is calculated as the time since its rebirth. I conducted preliminary analysis that showed reborn chains did not have different failure rates from other chains.

Motel. Motel is a dichotomous variable, and is coded 1 if the chain was substantially (more than 50% in terms of rooms) made up of motels. Each of the following features of a unit were treated as necessary and sufficient conditions for characterizing it as a motel:

- it had the word motel or court in its name;
- it had a name that would be appropriate for a motel (e.g., Rodeway Inn, or Hiway House);
- it was smaller than 150 rooms and part of a franchise commonly associated with motels (e.g., Holiday Inn or Howard Johnson's);
- it was smaller than 150 rooms and it was called a motor hotel or motor inn; or
- it was smaller than 150 rooms and located on a highway.

Further, chains whose units did not have 50% of their rooms in these units, but who had some of their rooms in such units, and the word "motel" in their name were coded as motel chains. The first motel chains appeared in the 1950s. Before 1950 there were motels, but they were typically owned independently, often by retirees (Young and Rubicam, Inc. 1948).

Franchisor. Franchisor is a dichotomous variable, and is coded 1 if the chain was a franchisor. Franchising is a relationship between two organizations where one (the franchisor) sells to the other (the franchisee) permission to use a brand name, and sometimes things that go with the brand name such as hotel architecture and management systems. A chain is treated as a franchisor if in the *Directory of Hotel Systems* it listed an executive responsible for franchising or franchisee relations, or if any one of its units was listed as a unit of another chain (the franchisee).

Referral System. Referral System is a dichotomous variable, and is coded 1 if the chain was a referral system. A referral system is a loose coupling of hotels that act in some ways like a chain. The hotels maintain independent ownership, but they may advertise jointly and use a centralized reservation system. For example, Best Western began as a referral system. Referral systems were noted as such in the *Directory of Hotel Systems*.

National Park. National Park is a dichotomous variable, and is coded 1 if the chain was associated with a national park. A chain was classified as associated with a national park if it had at least one unit with an address at a national park.

Log(Foreign Hotels). Foreign hotels are the number of hotels or motels not in one of the fifty U.S. states. So, Canadian, European, or even Puerto Rican hotels are counted as foreign. However, hotels in Alaska and Hawaii before they became states were treated as domestic.

Hotels Franchised. This is the number of hotels in the chain that are franchised from others. Hotels in a chain were identified as being franchised if they had a name associated with a franchisor (e.g., Holiday Inn, Days Inn, Ramada).

7

Mortality of Hotel Chains

The analysis of hotel chain mortality is important to this book in two ways. First, it provides an opportunity to analyze the impact of the environmental manipulations I have discussed. I have argued that changes in control systems, and in hotel management education were caused by chain entrepreneurs to help their organizations, and the hotel chain form. Here, I can test if those environmental changes made it easier for hotel chains to survive. Second, the mortality analysis can test the assertions I made about strategic advantages of chains. The arguments about advantages from economies of scale and repeated interactions imply that certain organizations should be more successful (survive longer) than others.

There has been a substantial amount of research using mortality studies to draw inferences regarding the effect of the environment on organizational forms. Environmental change is the focus of Carroll and Delacroix's (1982) study of the effect of political turmoil on newspaper mortality in Ireland and Argentina. In many other studies environmental change is controlled for. For example, Hannan and Freeman (1988) included period effects representing changes in the legal environment in a study of labor union mortality.

There is less research that uses mortality rates to study strategic advantages. The principal reason for this is probably that studying the effect of strategies requires organization-level information. This can be difficult to acquire across a population, over time. It may also be that strategic advantages have not been studied because of the skepticism that some organizational ecologists have regarding the ability of managers to adapt their organizations to strategic opportunities. If managers cannot change their organizations to meet opportunities, then advantages of organizations are uncontrollable (perhaps even random), and less interesting. Examples of mortality studies that test strategic arguments (or at least organization-level differences) are Freeman and Hannan (1983) on generalism and specialism among California restaurants, and Baum and Mezias (1992) on localized competition among Manhattan hotels.

I will begin by discussing the variables that test hypotheses in the mortality analysis. Then, I'll discuss some commonly used organization ecology variables, controls at the population-level, and controls at the organization-level. The discussion of variables will be followed by a description of the method, then results.

Variables That Test Hypotheses

Log(Hotels). This is the operationalization of organizational size. I have argued (chapter 3) that one of the reasons chains flourished was because there are economies of scale in the hospitality industry. A small chain has an economy of scale advantage over an independent hotel, and a large chain has an economy of scale advantage over a small chain. Hypothesis 1a states that larger chains will have lower mortality. A negative coefficient is predicted for Log(Hotels). There is another argument that results in a prediction for a negative coefficient for Log(Hotels). Larger organizations may have more slack resources than smaller ones. This would allow them to ride out periods of scarcity that would cause smaller organizations to fail (Freeman, Carroll and Hannan 1983). With the data available to me, I cannot separate the effect of slack from economies of scale in the coefficient of Log(Hotels). However, I have other tests of economy of scale arguments. Geographic concentration should increase economies of scale, but is unrelated to slack.

City Concentration. Economies of scale should be easier to reap for chains that are geographically concentrated. Such chains have less distance to ship material goods, move personnel, or cover with advertising. Hypothesis 1b states that geographically concentrated chains will have lower mortality. A negative coefficient is therefore predicted for City Concentration.

Regions. Regions is an alternative operationalization of geographic concentration. If the chain operates in more regions, it is less geographically concentrated, and according to hypothesis 1b will have a higher mortality rate. A positive coefficient is predicted for Regions.

Name Concentration. The arguments concerning the advantage of repeated interactions resulted in hypothesis 2, which predicted that chains with greater proportions of units with the same name will have lower mortality. Name Concentration is the proportion of units with the same name, and it should have a negative coefficient.

Log(Professional Managers). Chapter 4 described the process by which institutions changed and resulted in an increase in professional managers for the hospitality industry. Hotel chains rely on these managers and should become easier to operate (and less likely to fail) as the supply of managers increases. Hypothesis 3 predicts a negative coefficient for Log(Professional Managers).

Agency Cost. Chapter 5 described how control systems used by hotel chains increased in sophistication, and lowered agency costs. Hotel chains have a large separation between ownership and management, so lowering agency costs should reduce the risk of employee malfeasance and therefore the risk of chains failing. Hypothesis 5 predicts a positive coefficient for Agency Cost.

Traditional Organization Ecology Variables

Density and *Density^2*. There is an extensive literature regarding the effects of density on mortality (and founding) rates. In the theory of density dependence, density is argued to drive two forces that affect the critical rates of organizational populations: competition and legitimacy (Hannan and Freeman 1989). Competition, which increases the mortality rate, increases at an increasing rate with density. The number of possible competitive relationships in a group of organizations increases exponentially with the size of the group. Legitimacy, which decreases the mortality rate, increases at a decreasing rate. The earliest organizations of a form contribute greatly to the acceptance and familiarity of the form. Subsequent organizations contribute less.

These two influences on mortality combine to suggest a non-monotonic effect of density on mortality. As density first increases, increases in legitimacy dominate and the mortality rate falls. As density continues to increase a point is reached where increases in competition overwhelm increases in legitimacy, and mortality rates rise. Therefore, a negative coefficient is predicted for Density, and a positive coefficient for Density^2. The theory of density dependence was first tested on mortality rates by Hannan and Freeman (1988) in a study of the population of U.S. labor unions. Since then, it has been supported in numerous mortality studies.

Log(Age). The effect of age on organizational mortality is the subject of growing controversy. Initially, there was a near consensus that organizational mortality decreased with age. This position is referred to as the liability of newness, after Stinchcombe's (1965) argument that new organizations are at a disadvantage because they must establish roles and internal and external relationships. In mortality studies, the liability of newness is supported when the mortality rate decreases with age. Freeman et al. (1983) first demonstrated the liability of newness in a study of U.S. newspaper organizations, semiconductor firms and labor unions. Since then the liability of newness has been supported in studies on U.S. breweries, Manhattan banks and insurance companies (Hannan and Carroll 1992), and Toronto day care centers (Baum and Oliver 1991).

A refinement of the liability of newness position, referred to as the liability of adolescence, suggests that organizations may have a period of grace after their founding while they use up initial resources and appraise performance. The pattern of age dependence would then be non-monotonic. Mortality would be at first low, then increasing to a maximum. The age at which this maximum is reached depends on the population, and empirical findings range from six months (Brüderl and Schüssler 1990) to six years (Singh, House and Tucker 1986). After this peak is reached, mortality is argued to decrease with age. With the exception of the initial brief period, the liability of adolescence suggests the same decreasing age dependence as the liability of newness.

Recently a substantially different view, that organizations become antiquated as they age and mortality rates should increase, has been offered (Baum 1989; Ranger-Moore 1991; Ingram 1993b). The first challenge for this new position is to explain previous findings that support the liability of newness. A methodological problem, unobserved heterogeneity, is useful for this purpose. Unobserved heterogeneity essentially means that some variable that affects the transition (mortality) rate is left out of the model. This can explain findings of decreasing age dependence of mortality because the organizations that are disadvantaged on the unobserved variable will have higher mortality risks, and will die sooner. Other organizations will live longer, and because the reason they are advantaged is unobserved, it will seem that their mortality risk decreases with age. A strong candidate for the missing variable in previous liability of newness findings is organizational size. In a recent review, Baum (1996) finds that in fifteen studies that found decreasing age dependence, only two included temporaneous organizational size as a covariate (one other included size at the time of organizational founding). Of sixteen other mortality studies that included size, seven found no effect of age, six found increasing age dependence and three found non-monotonic effects of age. So, the liability of newness is almost never supported in studies that include organizational size. In the two instances where it is, it remains possible that some other important variable was excluded from the analysis.

If past findings of the liability of newness can be explained, it is still necessary to make an argument for positive age dependence. The seeds of such an argument are contained in the same essay by Stinchcombe (1965) that gave birth to the liability of newness. Stinchcombe argues there that organizations are imprinted with the environment (including technology, culture, and organizational practices) that exists at the time of their founding. If this is true (empirical support has been found by Carroll and Delacroix 1982 and Carroll and Hannan 1989) then organizations may become antiquated as time passes since their founding. Organizational technologies and the demands of environments change over time. As they do, old organizations may grow increasingly unfit, and their risk of mortality may increase. Of course, organizations may change as the environment changes, but there are inertial pressures (Hannan and Freeman 1984) that inhibit that ability. Further, organizational changes and reorganizations cause disturbances that can themselves raise mortality risks (Singh, Tucker and House 1986; Amburgey, Kelly and Barnett 1993).

A concrete example may clarify the antiquation argument. This study considers changes in control systems available to hotel chains. A chain formed in 1920 would be imprinted with the control technology of that time. Systems, procedures and relationships between organizational roles would be established at that time to exercise managerial control as it is understood. With time, control technology progresses. The chains being formed in 1930 will be organized using all the progress in control technology to that date. Therefore, they will have an advantage over a chain founded in 1920. The chain founded in 1920 is by 1930 ten years out of date. The older chain may try to adopt control advances, but this cannot be done without cost or risk. Changing established ways of operating creates uncertainty and confusion. Further, some control advances (for instance the use of a front-office posting machine) may have physical requirements that cannot be met by the hotels of an older chain. In fact, the aging of the fixed assets an organization starts with (in this case hotels) is another form of antiquation.

The antiquation argument suggests that the mortality rate will increase with a chain's age. It is also possible that the environment of hotel chains may be sufficiently slow changing that organizations can keep up with its demands, despite their inertia. In that case, there should be no effect of age on mortality. The use of log(Age) follows many other mortality studies, and is discussed in detail below.

Population-Level Control Variables

Occupancy. All private sector organizations (and most public ones) have cycles of resource munificence and scarcity. Some years are better than others. Many indicators of the U.S.'s economic health are to some extent informative for the hospitality industry. However, occupancy has the advantage of capturing the well-being of the industry with one variable. When the occupancy rate is high the industry is thriving, and chain mortality should be lower. When the occupancy rate is low, hotels (and chains of hotels) suffer financially, and chain mortality should be higher. A negative coefficient is predicted for occupancy.

Aggregate Chain Units. Hotel chains are made up of chain units. Chain units are often different from independent hotels. Independent hotels are generally smaller than chain units and are often not as well maintained. Therefore, Aggregate Chain Units may be seen as the level of a resource that hotel chains rely on. Chain mortality should decrease as chain hotels become more plentiful.

An alternative argument is that this variable represents the "mass" of the population. It has been suggested that the size of organizations may affect the legitimacy and competition that they generate (Barnett and Amburgey 1990). If that were true, mass should have the non-monotonic effect that density does. I tested and failed to find a non-monotonic effect by including the square of Aggregate Chain Units.

Independent Hotels. This represents the size of the population that most closely competes with hotel chains. Hannan and Freeman (1989) suggest that the Lotka-Volterra model of competitive interactions can be used to capture competitive (or mutualistic) relationships between populations of organizations. For the effect of independent hotels on chains the model is:

$$\frac{\partial N_c}{\partial t} = r_c \cdot N_c \left(\frac{K_c - \alpha_{c,i} \cdot N_i - N_c}{K_c} \right), \qquad (7\text{–}1)$$

where N_i is the density of independent hotels, N_c is the density of chains, r_c is the intrinsic growth rate of chains, $\alpha_{c,i}$ is the competition coefficient of independent hotels on chains, and K_c is the carrying capacity of chains (the equilibrium number of chains in the absence of competition). For competitive relationships, the competition coefficient would be positive. So, larger numbers of independent hotels should decrease the growth of the population of chains ($\partial N_c / \partial t$). The growth of the population of chains is not the subject of this analysis, but it is a function of founding and mortality. Precisely:

$$\frac{\partial N_c}{\partial t} = Chain\ Foundings_{\partial t} - Chain\ Deaths_{\partial t} \,. (7\text{–}2)$$

So, the mortality rate of chains should increase with the number of independent hotels (and the founding rate should decrease).

Aggregate Franchise Units. The growth of franchising represents one of the most important changes in the operating environment of hotel chains over the last 100 years. Different arguments can be made for the effect of increased franchising. First, franchising represents an increase in the pool of capital available for hotel chains. It makes it easier for individual citizens to invest in chains. This helps franchisees directly, but all chains indirectly by reducing the competition for capital from other sources.

Franchising also provides prototypes for organizing and operating hotel chains. Franchisors provide franchisees with extensive information and training about how to operate units (franchisors also monitor the operations of franchisees to make sure they meet standards). Again, this probably helps franchisees directly but indirectly contributes to the diffusion of organizing knowledge of this form, and helps all chains.

Fortunately, both of these effects of franchising imply the same thing for chain mortality. Franchising makes it easier to operate chains by generating capital, and providing templates for operation and organization. Therefore, the mortality rate of chains should decrease as franchising becomes more prevalent.

Chain-Level Control Variables

Motel. Motel chains and hotel chains may have different competitive patterns, and may be affected in different ways by environmental trends such as the establishment of interstate highways. There are potential advantages for both hotel and motel chains and it is not clear which should have a lower mortality rate. However, even though I have no prediction for the effect of being a motel chain on the mortality rate, it is important statistically to control for possible differences between the mortality rates of hotel and motel chains. This control is achieved by including the Motel variable in the analysis.

Franchisor. Hotel chains probably become franchisors because they have a better than average operating system and market position. But, there are unique demands to franchising such as the monitoring of franchisees. I have no prediction for the effect of being a franchisor on mortality and therefore include the Franchisor variable as a control.

Referral System. Because referral systems are "loosely coupled," with diverse ownership, they probably have political battles over direction. Further, the members have low investment, and can easily withdraw from the system. Therefore, referral systems should have higher mortality rates.

National Park. Being associated with a National Park represents an institutional linkage. Baum and Oliver (1992) have argued that institutional linkages decrease mortality. I suspect that the resource implications of association with a National Park outweigh legitimacy benefits. National Parks consistently attract large numbers of tourists, and they regulate the number of hotels with access to those tourists. Because of the advantage of access to tourists, chains associated with National Parks should have lower mortality rates.

Log(Foreign Hotels). Foreign hotels are units that are not included in the size variable. Also, having foreign hotels may increase the status of a chain. But there are costs to operating a multi-national organization. I have no prediction for the effect of the number of foreign hotels on mortality.

Hotels Franchised. Again, there are advantages and disadvantages to franchising hotels from others. The franchisee gets an established marketing concept and a set of operating procedures. Franchising also addresses the agency problem. Essentially, it is a mechanism to sell the worker (or manager) the firm. But, these things must be paid for, and the franchisor typically maintains the power to end the franchise agreements, and kill the franchisee's chain. I have no prediction for the effect of the number of hotels franchised on mortality.

Table 7-1 shows a correlation matrix for these variables.

METHOD

Definition of a Chain Death

A significant problem in a study of organizational mortality is defining death. Organizations may change their form or they may cease operations but persist as legal entities. If they do cease to exist, they may do so for a number of reasons. They can be absorbed by another organization, they can merge with another, or they may simply fail and disband. Hannan and

Table 7–1
Correlations of Variables in Mortality Analysis

	(1)	(2)	(3)	(4)	(5)	(6)	(7)	(8)	(9)	(10)	(11)	(12)	(13)	(14)	(15)	(16)	(17)	(18)	(19)
(1) Density	1.0	.96	.03	-.09	.69	.85	.79	.37	.13	.09	-.05	.12	.27	.21	-.18	.18	.31	-.85	.77
(2) Density^2		1.0	-.01	-.07	.61	.91	.91	.40	.14	.10	-.05	.12	.31	.21	-.19	.18	.36	-.76	.61
(3) Log(Age)			1.0	-.05	.12	-.02	-.06	-.15	.07	-.06	.13	.13	-.10	.17	.01	.14	-.13	-.10	.10
(4) Occupancy				1.0	-.48	-.30	-.18	-.22	-.09	-.06	-.00	-.11	-.08	-.11	.05	-.08	-.20	.14	-.40
(5) Independent Hotels					1.0	.69	.48	.37	.15	.10	-.02	.16	.19	.19	-.12	.18	.32	-.88	.66
(6) Aggregate Chain Units						1.0	.95	.49	.18	.13	-.04	.16	.34	.24	-.19	.20	.45	-.71	.55
(7) Aggregate Franchise Units							1.0	.44	.16	.11	-.03	.13	.35	.21	-.18	.18	.42	-.54	.40
(8) Motel								1.0	.21	.25	-.06	.09	.34	.31	-.26	.21	.45	-.34	.25
(9) Franchisor									1.0	-.02	-.02	.42	-.01	.52	-.21	.47	.29	-.13	.10
(10) Referral System										1.0	-.02	.15	-.02	.22	-.09	.02	-.04	-.09	.07
(11) National Park											1.0	-.01	-.03	-.02	.19	-.10	-.10	.04	-.05
(12) Log(Foreign Hotels)												1.0	.01	.49	-.20	.51	.16	-.13	.10
(13) Hotels Franchised													1.0	.18	-.16	.18	.24	-.20	.15
(14) Log(Hotels)														1.0	-.48	.79	.14	-.19	.18
(15) City Concentration															1.0	-.55	-.24	.15	-.14
(16) Regions																1.0	.23	-.18	.14
(17) Name Concentration																	1.0	-.28	.18
(18) Log(Professional Managers)																		1.0	-.72
(19) Agency Cost																			1.0

Freeman(1989) argue that different influences explain the different ending events. For example, successful organizations make good targets for absorption while unsuccessful organizations fail.

My definition of a hotel chain relies on operations and has nothing to do with legal form, so I avoid the problem of "lingering death" when legal organizations cease operations. Transitions such as a change in top management, region of operation, or hotel/motel strategy were not treated as ending events. Changes in ownership were not treated as ending events as long as the organization continued operations. This treatment was mainly because organizations change ownership frequently with little relationship to the success of their operations (consider public companies) but also because the available data on changes in ownership were incomplete.

When chains ended I tracked the subsequent ownership of their hotels to determine the nature of the ending event. There were no mergers of equal strength chains. If another chain ended up with more than one-half of the ending chain's hotels the ending event was coded as an absorption. If the chain ceased to operate three hotels and was not absorbed it was coded as a failure. The goal of this analysis is to explain the rise of hotel chains, and absorptions don't contribute to this because they only reallocate chain units between organizations rather than changing the overall size of the chain population. So, the ending events I model are failures. Absorptions were infrequent (there were 620 failures and only 31 absorptions) and were treated as right censored in the analysis (Hannan and Freeman 1988).

Models

Chain mortality was modeled using r(t), the instantaneous rate of mortality. This hazard rate of mortality is defined as the limiting probability of a death between t and t + Δt, given that the chain was alive at t, calculated over Δt:

$$r(t) = \lim_{\Delta t \to 0} Pr\left(\frac{(death\ t,\ t+\Delta t \mid alive\ at\ t)}{\Delta t} \right). \quad (7\text{–}3)$$

Figure 7–1 shows a plot of the chain mortality hazard rate (determined using the Nelson-Aalen method) against the year.

Parametric estimates of the hazard rate require assumptions about the effect of time (in these models, age) on mortality (Tuma and Hannan 1984). Graphic and statistical methods were used to arrive at assumptions regarding the parametric representation of age dependence (Hannan 1988). Support was found for a power function age dependence. This is the conventional

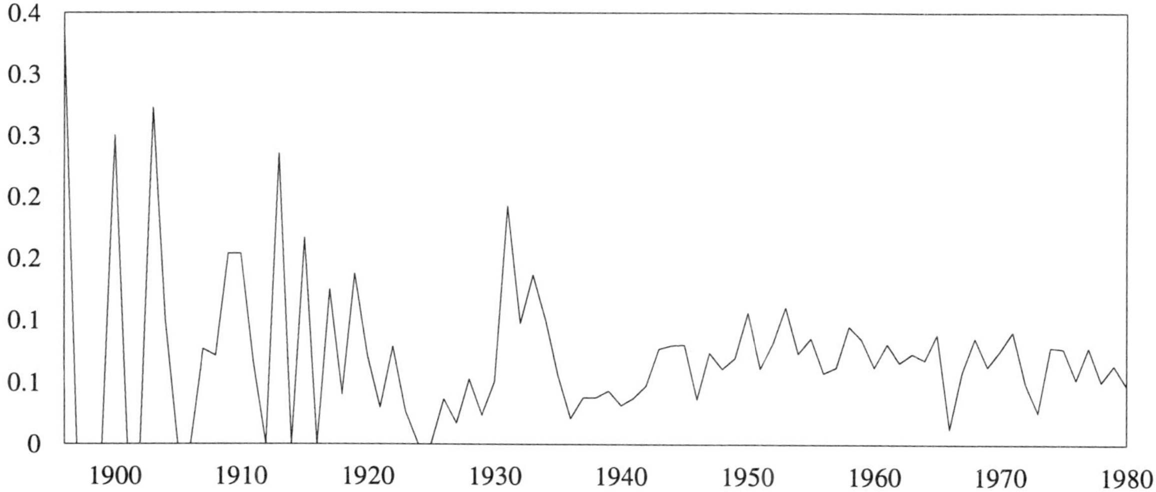

Figure 7-1. Nelson-Aalen Hazard Rate for Hotel Chain Mortality.

parameterization of age dependence in studies of organizational mortality. Power function age dependence is modeled with a Weibull model:

$$r(t) = e^{\beta X} e^{\tau \log(t)}, \qquad (7\text{–}4)$$

where β is a vector of coefficients, x is a vector of covariates, τ is the coefficient for age and t represents age. The reported results are maximum-likelihood estimates obtained using the Lifereg procedure of the SAS statistical package. Additional analysis (not presented) was performed using the piecewise exponential model and the statistical package TDA (Rohwer, 1993). The piecewise exponential model is a particularly flexible approach to modeling age dependence. The results of this additional analysis were comparable to those presented here on all substantive dimensions.

Table 7–2 shows four nested models. All models include Log(Hotels) because this size measure appears to be a critical determinant of mortality. Model 1 also includes the traditional organizational ecology variables of density and age. Model 2 adds the population-level control variables. Model 3 adds chain-level control variables. Finally, Model 4 adds the variables that test hypotheses. Table 7–3 shows a statistical comparison of the nested models. Each set of variables significantly adds to the power of the model. Therefore, the discussion of results will rely on the full model, Model 4.

RESULTS

Log(Hotels) tests hypothesis 1a, that larger chains will have lower mortality rates due to economies of scale. The coefficient is negative and significant (-1.90, $p < .01$), so larger chains do have lower mortality rates, and hypothesis 1a is supported. Hypothesis 1b also addresses economies of scale, and suggests that geographically concentrated chains will have lower mortality rates. Two variables test this hypothesis. City Concentration is negative and significant (-.55, $p < .01$) indicating that chains that are more concentrated in one city have lower mortality. Regions is positive and significant (0.142, $p < .01$) indicating that chains that operate in more regions have higher mortality. Both these results support hypothesis 1b.

Hypothesis 2, that chains that can establish repeated interactions will have lower mortality, is tested with Name Concentration. That variable is negative and significant (-.50, $p < .01$). This indicates that chains which have a greater proportion of units named in a consistent way, and which are therefore better able to establish repeated interactions, have lower mortality. Hypothesis 2 is supported.

Table 7–2
Weibull Models of Hotel Chain Mortality, 1896–1980
Coefficients Represent Effects on Log-Hazard

Variable	(1)	(2)	(3)	(4)
Constant	-.875 **	0.819 +	0.85 +	2.044 +
	(.23)	(.63)	(.65)	(1.5)
Density	0.004 *	-.006 +	-.006 +	.0194 **
	(.002)	(.004)	(.004)	(.007)
Density^2	-6.0E-6	0.42E-4 *	0.4E-4 *	0.7E-7
	(.000)	(.000)	(.000)	(.000)
Log(Age)	0.0085	0.008	0.02	0.03
	(.02)	(.02)	(.02)	(.03)
Occupancy	—	-.017 **	-.017 **	-.02 *
		(.006)	(.006)	(.009)
Independent Hotels	—	-.007 *	-.007 +	0.007
		(.004)	(.004)	(.007)
Aggregate Chain Units	—	0.0001	0.0001	0.0002 *
		(.000)	(.004)	(.000)
Aggregate Franchise Units		-.002 **	-.002 **	-.003 **
		(.001)	(.001)	(.000)
Motel	—	—	-.314 *	-.233 +
			(.16)	(.17)
Franchisor	—	—	1.00 +	1.10 +
			(.72)	(.74)

* Continued on following page.

One-tailed test of significance: + < .10, * < .05, ** < .01.

Table 7–2 (Continued)
Weibull Models of Hotel Chain Mortality, 1896–1980
Coefficients Represent Effects on Log-Hazard

Variable	(1)	(2)	(3)	(4)
Referral System	—	—	2.69 **	2.65 **
			(.63)	(.64)
National Park	—	—	-2.78 **	-2.6 **
			(1.0)	(1.0)
Log(Foreign Hotels)	—	—	-.048	-.079
			(.07)	(.08)
Hotels Franchised	—	—	0.042 *	0.045 *
			(.03)	(.03)
Log(Hotels)	-1.49 **	-1.49 **	-1.56 **	-1.90 **
	(.11)	(.11)	(.12)	(.14)
City Concentration	—	—	—	-.55 **
				(.16)
Regions	—	—	—	0.142 **
				(.06)
Name Concentration	—	—	—	-.50 **
				(.20)
Log(Professional Managers)		—	—	-.304 **
				(.08)
Agency Cost	—	—	—	0.014 **
				(.004)
Log-Likelihood	-2158.9	-2154.2	-2134.2	-2108.2
Spells	9606	9606	9606	9606
Events	620	620	620	620

One-tailed test of significance: + < .10, * < .05, ** < .01.

Table 7–3
Comparison of Nested Weibull Models from Table 7–2

Model	Added Variables	Log-likelihood	Log-likelihood Ratio of Comparison to Previous Model	Significance of Chi-Squared Test
(0)	Restricted-Slopes (1)	-2335.1	-	-
(1)	Organizational Ecology (4)	-2158.9	352.4	< .001
(2)	Environmental Controls (4)	-2154.2	9.4	< .10
(3)	Chain Level Controls (6)	-2134.2	50.0	< .001
(4)	Hypotheses Testing (5)	-2108.2	52.0	< .001

Log(Professional Managers) tests hypothesis 3, that chain mortality decreases as the supply of professional managers increases. Log(Professional Managers) is significant and negative (-.304, $p < .01$). Hypothesis 3 is supported. Of course, this statistical finding says nothing about the cause of the increase in professional managers. As I have explained, I rely on historical evidence to show that hotel chain entrepreneurs manipulated the institutional environment to generate a supply of the managers they required. The causal relationship between the supply of managers and chain mortality, and an alternative operationalization of the supply of professional managers, are addressed later in this chapter.

The other hypothesis about the effect of an environmental manipulation on mortality, hypothesis 5, is tested using Agency Cost. Agency Cost is positive and significant (0.014, $p < .01$). The mortality rate is positively related to agency cost. So, when agency cost falls because of changes in the control systems available to hotel chains, chain mortality also falls. Hypothesis 5 is supported.

Turning to the traditional organizational ecology variables, Density is positive and significant (.0194, $p < .01$) but Density^2 is not significant. The non-monotonic relationship proposed by the theory of density dependence is not found. In Models 2 and 3 density has the predicted non-monotonic effect on failure, but when the variables of substantive interest are added in Model 4, the effect of density becomes monotonically increasing. Table 7–1 shows that there is a high correlation (-.85) between Log(Professional Managers) and Density. This suggests a possibility of multicolinearity between those two variables, which may account for the failure of Model 4 to show a non-monotonic effect of density.

Log(Age) was not significant. This is consistent with the implication of the antiquation argument in a slow changing environment. In models (not shown) that excluded Log(Hotels), Log(Age) was negative and significant. This supports the contention that past findings in support of the liability of newness resulted from unobserved heterogeneity due to the exclusion of size measures.

As expected, mortality rates were lower when occupancy rates were higher (-.02, $p <.05$). Surprisingly, the effect of Independent Hotels is not significant. I expected it to be positive, indicating competition between independent hotels and chains. This could be because of the sub-optimal measurement of Independent Hotels. It could also be that more localized tests of inter-population competition (perhaps at the state level) are necessary. Aggregate Chain Units was positive and significant (.0002, $p < .05$). This goes against my prediction, and supports the idea that Aggregate

Chain Units represents mass, and that its increase causes an increase in competition. I estimated a model (not shown) with Aggregate Chain Units^2 to check for a non-monotonic effect. That variable did have a weakly significant negative coefficient ($-3.37*10^{-08}$, $p < .10$) but the combined effect of Aggregate Chain Units and Aggregate Chain Units^2 was *strictly increasing* (although at a decreasing rate) over the period of this study. The final population-level control variable, Aggregate Franchise Units, was negative and significant (-.003, $p < .01$). As expected, mortality decreases as franchising becomes more prevalent.

Being a Motel chain had a significant negative effect on the mortality rate (-.233, $p < .10$). Being a Franchisor had a significant positive effect on the mortality rate (1.10, $p < .10$). As expected Referral Systems had higher mortality rates (2.69, $p < .01$), and chains associated with National Parks had lower mortality rates (-2.6, $p < .01$). The effect of Log(Foreign Hotels) was not significant. The final chain-level control, Hotels Franchised, was positive and significant (0.045, $p < .05$) indicating that franchisees have higher mortality rates.

ISSUES AND REFINEMENTS OF THE MORTALITY ANALYSIS

Multicolinearity and Spurious Correlation

The two variables that represent environmental changes, Agency Cost and Log(Professional Managers), are time series with a trend (Agency Cost decreases and Log[Professional Managers] increases over time). A number of other variables, such as Aggregate Franchise Units, Independent Hotels, Aggregate Chain Units, Density and Density^2 are also time series with trends. Two concerns are raised by this. First, there could be multicolinearity. Second, perhaps the significant coefficients of Agency Cost and Log(Professional Managers) are the result of spurious correlation between variables with time trends.

The correlations in Table 7–1 show that although there are strong correlations between many of the time series, the correlations are not so strong for the time series which I am most interested in. Agency Cost has no correlations larger than .80 and Log(Professional Managers) is strongly correlated (>.80) only with Density and Independent Hotels. Further, in the various models I estimated (many not shown) the coefficients of the environmental time-series variables were stable with the exception of the change in the estimated effect of Density and Independent Hotels when

Log(Professional Managers) was included in Model 4. There is a possibility that the estimated effects of Density and Independent Hotels in Model 4 result from multicolinearity, but the stability of the other coefficients indicate that multicolinearity does not effect them. Finally, as Figure 7–1 shows, there is a lot of variance in the mortality rate of hotel chains over time. The rate is obviously highly sensitive to changes in its determinants, and this made it possible to get good estimates despite the presence of a number of environmental time series. For these reasons, I do not feel multicolinearity was a serious problem in these models although a caution regarding the interpretation of the coefficients of Density and Independent Hotels is warranted..

Regarding spurious correlation, recognize that the time trends in the variables that represent environmental manipulation are the subject of theoretical attention in this study. I've presented two chapters of history to explain why agency costs fell and the supply of professional managers increased. The statistical analysis was motivated by *a priori* hypotheses, and was not exploratory. Further, although there are general trends in both Agency Cost and Log(Professional Managers), neither variable changes monotonically. The supply of professional managers is constant at zero until 1925, and decreases during World War II. As Figure 5–1 showed, Agency Cost increased during the depression. Perhaps more importantly, the dependent variable, the mortality rate, is anything but monotonic (see Figure 7–1). It has a slight downward trend over 100 years of observation, but it increases many times. Finally, there are other time series with trends in the same direction as the environmental-manipulation variables, but with estimated coefficients in the opposite direction. For example, Density, Aggregate Chain Units, and Log(Professional Managers) all tend to increase over the period of observation. But Density and Aggregate Chain Units have positive coefficients, while Log(Professional Managers) has a negative coefficient. An argument of spurious correlation is unconvincing when significant coefficients are found in directions opposite to those suggested by time trends.

Causality and the Supply of Professional Managers

Significant results in an analysis of this type do not evidence the direction of causality. One variable in particular, Log(Professional Managers), appears susceptible to an argument that reverses the causality as I have presented it. I have argued that hotel chains flourished (failed less and were founded more) partly because they were able to manipulate increases in the supply of professional managers. It could be that the supply of professional managers was pulled by the number of hotel chains: hotel chains exist without concern for the supply of managers, and the supply adjusts to the number of chains. Three arguments cause me to reject this alternative explanation of causality in the relationship between chain mortality and the supply of professional managers.

First, this analysis (and those in the following chapters) is dynamic. The dependent variable is not the number of hotel chains, but rather the number of chain deaths (in the next chapter, chain foundings). So, for the alternative causal explanation to hold, it would be necessary for the supply of professional managers to adjust not to the size of the chain population, but to the number of chain deaths in a year. It seems unlikely that educators and students could so effectively predict the dynamics of the hotel chain population.

Second, I have provided evidence of the original direction of causality. Initially, hotel schools were established by chain entrepreneurs who required managers. After that point, it is likely that the control of chain entrepreneurs over the resource decreased. Now hotel schools operate with a fair degree of autonomy: they are no longer "servants" of hotel chains. But, such an evolution of an institutional arrangement is not unexpected. North (1990) notes that institutions are path dependent. Institutions define incentives, and therefore actors can be expected to align themselves with the existing arrangement. The magnetic attraction of interests to institutions causes the institutions to be inertial. For instance, faculty, staff and alumni develop an interest in the Cornell Hotel School. Once the school is established it becomes a vehicle through which they satisfy their interests. They can be expected to fight to ensure it continues to serve them.

Third, I have performed an analysis to reject the alternative causal argument. If it were true that the supply of managers did not drive chain success, but was simply pulled along by that success then a lag of the Occupancy variable (which summarizes the environmental munificence for chains) should be an effective predictor of mortality (perhaps more than Log(Professional Managers)). If the hospitality industry was thriving, potential hotel mangers would recognize it, and about five years later the supply of managers should increase. Table 7–4 shows the results of a number of alternative estimations of the full model discussed above. For ease of presentation, it shows only the variables of substantive interest (there were no notable changes in the control variables). Model 4 is simply the full model from Table 7–2. Model 5 is the full model with the addition of Occupancy lagged 5 years. The model is not a significant improvement over

Table 7–4
Alternate Estimations of Hotel Chain Mortality, 1896–1980
Coefficients Represent Effects on Log-Hazard

Variable	Full Model (4)	5 Year Lag of Occupancy (5)	Stock of Professional Managers (6)	Gamma Estimation (7)
Coefficients of Control Variables Are Not Shown				
Log(Hotels)	-1.90 ** (.14)	-1.90 ** (.14)	-1.90 ** (.14)	-.279 ** (.030)
City Concentration	-.55 ** (.16)	-.56 ** (.16)	-.56 ** (.16)	-.070 + (.05)
Regions	0.142 ** (.06)	0.142 ** (.06)	0.143 ** (.06)	0.038 ** (.01)
Name Concentration	-.50 ** (.20)	-.50 ** (.20)	-.50 ** (.20)	-.092 * (.05)
Log(Professional Managers)	-.304 ** (.08)	-.296 ** (.08)	—	-.059 * (.03)
Agency Cost	0.014 ** (.004)	0.016 ** (.004)	0.018 ** (.004)	0.002 * (.001)
Lag(Occupancy)	—	0.010 (.008)	—	—
Log(Stock Professional Mangers)		—	-.283 ** (.08)	—
Gamma Shape Parameter		—	—	-2.913
Log-Likelihood	-2108.2	-2107.87	-2108.74	-1415.0
Spells	9606	9606	9606	9606
Events	620	620	620	620

One-tailed test of significance: + < .10, * < .05, ** < .01.

Model 4 ($\chi^2_{1df} = 0.66$, $p \approx .40$). Lag(Occupancy) is not significant, and all the substantive variables are unchanged. Therefore, there is not evidence that the supply of managers simply responds to the fortunes of the population of chains, rather than being manipulated by chains and chain entrepreneurs and contributing to the success of chains.

Stock Vs. Flow of Professional Managers

As noted in chapter 6, the use of Cornell Hotel School graduates in a year is only a proxy for the extent of professional management in the hospitality industry. There are few alternative operationalizations of professional management, but one obvious one is that professional management could be a different function of the number of Cornell Hotel School graduates. Specifically, the total number of past graduates in the workforce may more accurately represent professional management than the size of the class in any one year. The "stock" of Cornell graduates may be a better proxy than the "flow."

Certainly the contribution of hotel schools to professional management includes past graduates as well as the current class. On the other hand, over time many hotel school graduates probably move to other industries. Further, mortality and founding rates represent marginal changes in the chain population. Perhaps they are best predicted by marginal changes in managerial resources (flow). In any case, it is worthwhile to compare both operationalizations. Model 6 in Table 7–4 estimates the full model using Log(Stock of Professional Managers) rather than Log(Flow of Professional Managers) that is used in Model 4. Most importantly the stock variable is significant in the predicted direction (-.283, $p < .01$). Whether the stock or flow operationalization is used, hypothesis 3 is still supported. Although Model 4 and Model 6 are not nested, Model 4 (with the flow operationalization) has a slightly larger χ^2: -2108.2 vs. -2108.74. Therefore, the flow of professional managers will continue to be used in subsequent analyses.

Unobserved Heterogeneity and a Gamma Estimation

I have explained the problem of unobserved heterogeneity, and that it almost certainly exists when size is omitted from a mortality model. Although size is included here, countless other variables that may affect chain mortality are not. For example, environmental variables such as the interest rate, miles of interstate highway, and the number of campgrounds; and chain-level variables such as top management characteristics, presence of centralized reservation systems, or cash management strategy may affect the mortality rate. It could be asked if my results would stand up if all these omitted variables were included.

Fortunately, there is a way to test the implications of unobserved variables using the gamma distribution. The gamma distribution is extremely flexible, ranging from a highly skewed J-shape to a nearly symmetric unimodal shape depending on the values of its parameters. This makes it useful for social scientists trying to capture the unpredictable effects of unobserved covariates. Tuma and Hannan (1984) suggest adding a multiplicative disturbance with a gamma distribution to the model for the hazard rate. I use an alternative that introduces a gamma-distributed disturbance into the waiting time version of the hazard model (Hannan 1988). This allows for a rigorous test of my hypotheses. Essentially, the gamma estimated model gives structure to the error term in a way designed to best account for the effects of all omitted variables.

Model 7 in Table 7–4 shows the gamma estimated version of the full model. Most importantly, every variable of substantive interest remains significant in the predicted direction (significance levels generally fall, but remain within conventional levels). The size of the effects for each variable becomes smaller. This is to be expected, especially since the variables that test hypotheses are proxies for underlying concepts (for instance, if all the other variables that capture changes in agency cost were included, the coefficient of the fidelity bonding rate would surely be smaller). Summarizing, even when the estimated effects of all omitted variables are included, all of the hypotheses are supported.

DISCUSSION OF MORTALITY RESULTS

Models of mortality rates provided support for all hypotheses. Chains were found to benefit from economies of scale, and from the ability to participate in repeated interactions with customers. The environmental manipulations that chain entrepreneurs engaged in caused reductions in the mortality rates of chains.

It is worthwhile to consider the magnitude of the effects of the environmental manipulations of hotel chain entrepreneurs. As noted, the coefficients presented represent the effect on the log-hazard. It is simple to convert them to effects on the hazard. For instance, the Log(Hotels) coefficient can be interpreted as:

Mortality Rate = Mortality Rate * exp(-1.90 * Log(Hotels)); (7–6)

alternatively, the percentage change in the mortality rate is:

% change in the rate = exp (-1.90 * Log(Hotels)) - 1. (7–7)

Because the models are multiplicative the effect of any variable depends on the level of other variables. However, (7–6) shows that the rate can be separated into a "ceteris-paribus" component and a multiplier, called the multiplier of the rate, that captures the influences of a specific variable.

Figure 7–2 shows how the multiplier of the rate for Log(Professional Managers) changes over time. The graph begins in 1925 with the first Cornell Hotel School graduates. Before that time Log(Professional Managers) was constant at Log(0.1) and the multiplier of the rate was constant at 2.01. Therefore, because of the operationalization of the supply of professional managers there was a sudden drop in the mortality rate of chains in 1925, with the first Cornell graduates. However, there is still a substantial effect on the mortality rate in the period after 1925. The multiplier of the rate is 0.5294 in 1925, and 0.1929 in 1980. So a chain in 1900 was about ten times (2.01 / .1929) as likely to fail as a chain in 1980 controlling for all else but the change in professional managers. A chain in 1925 was 2.75 times (.5294 / .1929) as likely to fail as a chain in 1980. The multiplier of the rate due to the supply of professional managers increases during World War II when there was a shortage of labor for service industries.

Figure 7–3 shows the multiplier of the rate for Agency Cost over time. Here, the effect is even more striking than with Log(Professional Managers). The multiplier of the rate in 1896 is 17.4. By 1980 it falls to 1.52. So a chain in 1896 was 11.5 times as likely to fail as a chain in 1980 controlling for all else but the change in Agency Cost. The two environmental manipulations together account for a decrease in the mortality rate of chains between 1896 and 1980 of more than 99%.

The results of control variables are also useful for understanding the rise of hotel chains. The monotonically increasing effect of density on failure in Model 4 indicates that hotel chains do not have the same population dynamics that are found in many other populations of organizations (although this is not conclusive because of the possibility of multicolinearity described above). It appears that hotel chains suffer competition from increases in the number of other hotel chains, but do not enjoy a benefit of increased legitimacy. The simplest explanation for this would be that there

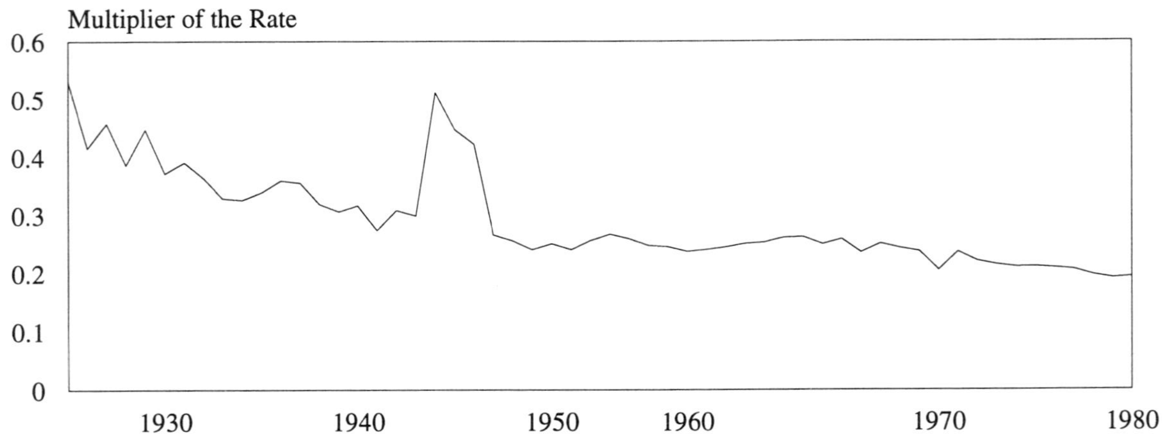

Figure 7-2.
Effect of Changes in the Supply of Professional Managers on the Morality Rate.
Uses the coefficient from Model 4 (-.296) for Log(Professional Managers).

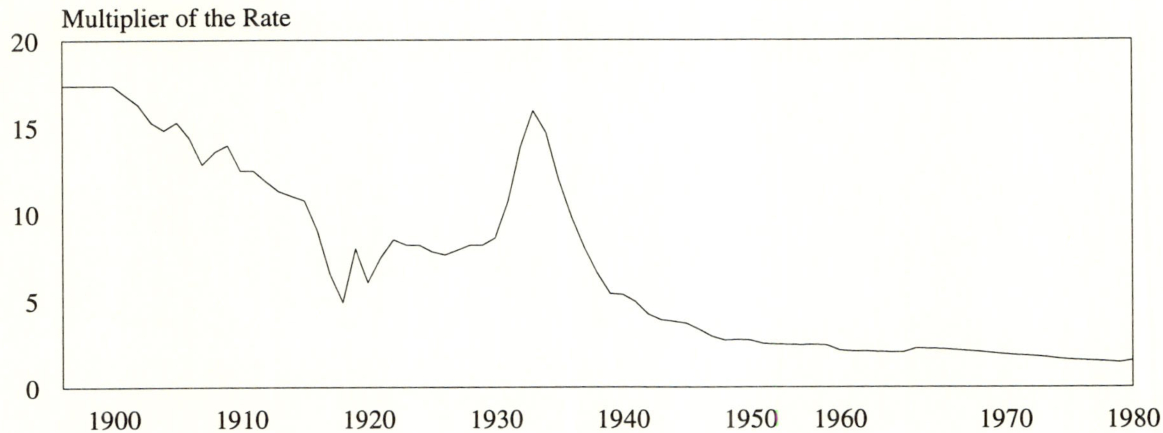

Figure 7-3.
Effect of Changes in Agency Cost on the Mortality Rate.
Using the coefficient (0.014) for Agency Cost from Model 4.

is no density driven increase in legitimacy for this population. That seems at least feasible because hotels and chain organizations both existed, and had presumably gained legitimacy, before this population began. Evidence from the early years of hotel chains, however, indicates that legitimacy was in question. A 1938 advertisement for American Hotels notes that "any sort of 'chain' is ordinarily a cold and unattractive thing" (Hotel Redbook 1938). A 1910 editorial of the Western Hotel Reporter (July 9, 5) argued that hotel chains would not succeed because "American hotel managers were much too individualistic to follow one master policy or system."

It is possible that while legitimacy was at first low and is now high, it did not grow as a function of density. Also, it seems likely that competition between chains may be regionally determined. Localized density measures (Baum and Mezias 1992) may yield results consistent with the theory of density dependence. Finally, it has been argued that non-monotonic density effects on mortality can be explained without using legitimacy (Levinthal 1991). As technologies improve, firm's prices may fall, and their points of efficient scale may change. As prices fall, quantity demanded increases and the carrying capacity for the firm increases. But, as efficient scale increases each firm supplies more, and the carrying capacity for the firm decreases. Depending on the shape of demand and cost curves, increasing, decreasing, or non-monotonic effects of density on mortality are possible.

Competition within the population of hotel chains is also indicated by the coefficient of Aggregate Chain Units, which represents the mass of the population. Barnett and Amburgey (1990) argue that when density is controlled for, the coefficient of population mass indicates the effect of increasing the size of other organizations on the failure rate of the focal organization. The positive effect of mass on failure could therefore be interpreted as evidence that larger chains generate more competition.

Although I had no prediction for the effect of being a motel chain, it is notable that those chains had lower rates of failure. The transition of organization in the hospitality industry in the twentieth century is not only from independent hotel to chain, but also increasingly from hotel to motel. Part of the advantage of motel chains is likely due to the increasing importance of automobile travel. Another explanation for the growing success of motels may be that motels entered the hospitality industry after hotels, and therefore had the opportunity to learn vicariously from the experience of hotels. Consistent with the advantage of motel chains over hotel chains, Ingram and Inman (1997) find that individual motels have lower failure rates than individual hotels at Niagara Falls.

Another chain type, referral systems, had higher failure rates. The weakness of the referral system form of chain may be explained by transaction cost economics. The transaction costs of a chain organization where units have multiple owners are very likely higher than the transaction costs of a traditional chain. In a referral system, within-chain transactions are much more complicated because they are between different owners. For example, consider a customer who has a bad experience at a chain hotel. The customer might be appeased with a coupon for a free stay at another hotel of the chain. If the chain is a traditional chain, such a transaction is easy because the hotel that provided the poor service and the hotel that will provide the redress are owned by the same person or persons. In a referral system, however, those two hotels have different owners and some further compensation between the hotel that provided the bad service and the hotel that provides the redress is probably necessary to satisfy all parties. Besides the problem of within-chain transactions, referral systems also have additional complications surrounding decision making. The legal structure of a referral system resembles a partnership, and for any decision there are numerous partners who may favor different alternatives. A voting process may result in a decision, but if the decision requires the support of all members of the referral system, its implementation may be inhibited.

Franchising is an important practice in the hotel industry, and the failure results indicate that it affected the rise of hotel chains. The failure rate of chains is lower as the aggregate level of franchising increases, but specific chains that are franchisees have higher failure rates. Franchisors also have higher failure rates. So, the practice of franchising provides a general benefit to the population of hotel chains, but hurts the chains that are directly involved with franchising. This suggests that franchising provides a resource, such as increased sources of financing, that trickles through the whole chain population, not just the organizations directly engaged in franchising.

An important question prompted by the failure results is why chains engage in franchising at all, given that it increases their failure rate. It may be that franchising benefits chains in other ways. For franchisors, it is very likely that franchising helps them grow faster since it increases the capacity of entrepreneurs to control the organization by assigning strong incentives to franchisee managers. The analysis of chain growth reported in chapter 9 of this book does not estimate an effect for being a franchisor since the type of dynamic model used cannot estimate effects on growth for features of the chain that do not change over the life of the chain. Ingram (1996), however, uses a different method to estimate chain growth and does find that franchisors grow much more quickly than other chains. For franchisees, the benefit may be the expertise to operate a hotel chain. Since franchising typically involves a transfer of an operating system from the franchisor to the franchisee, it is reasonable to assume that being a franchisee is more appealing to entrepreneurs who lack expertise in the hotel industry. If the alternative is not operating a hotel chain at all, then being a franchisee with a higher risk of failure but with some potential for profit, may appeal to entrepreneurs without hospitality expertise. The role of franchising as a determinant of organizational form in the hospitality industry deserves further study.

Finally, the result that chains associated with national parks have lower failure rates supports the limited past evidence that linkages to the state help organizations (Baum and Oliver 1992). Very few chains were associated with national parks, but those that were had a substantial survival advantage. The coefficient from Model 4 of -2.6 indicates that chains associated with national parks had a failure rate 0.074 times that of other chains. The benefit of national parks for chains suggests that parks may be another area where hospitality entrepreneurs may pursue their interests through institutional change. Ingram and Inman (1997) document the efforts of hoteliers at Niagara Falls to create the parks there, and the subsequent benefit to hospitality organizations.

8

Foundings of Hotel Chains

For studies of organizational founding, the unit of analysis cannot be the (potential) organization because of the impossibility of defining the risk set. The set of social actors that are at risk of founding a hotel chain is undefined. A larger, definable, unit of analysis must be used. The population of the organizational form is an appropriate unit of analysis. So, the rate at which hotel chains are founded in the U.S. will be estimated. Figure 8–1 shows this rate.

Because the founding rate is modeled at the population level, chain-level factors (such as the strategy for naming units) cannot be included. However, all of the population-level variables used in the mortality analysis can be and are used here. Predictions for their effects on founding are the opposite of predictions for their effects on mortality, so I will describe them briefly.

Variables that Test Hypotheses

Log(Professional Managers). The founding rate of chains should increase with the supply of professional managers because professional managers are a resource that facilitates the successful operation of a chain (hypothesis 4).

Agency Cost. Operating a chain is more inviting when agency costs are lower because losses from employee malfeasance are lower. Therefore, the founding rate should be negatively related to Agency Cost. As Agency Cost falls due to changes in control systems, founding rates will increase (hypothesis 6).

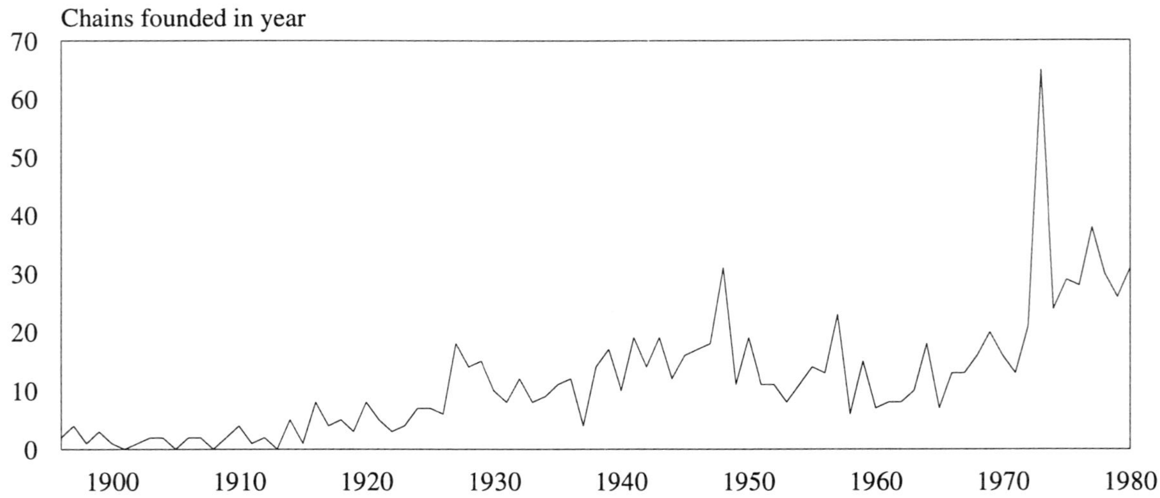

Figure 8-1. Founding Rate for Hotel Chains.

Traditional Organizational Ecology Variables

Density and *Density²*. The theory of density dependence suggests that Density should have a positive effect on founding, and Density² should have a negative effect. Foundings should increase as legitimacy increases, and then decrease as competition overwhelms legitimacy gains.

Population Level Controls

Occupancy. Founding rates should be positively related to the occupancy rate. The occupancy rate represents the economic health of the hospitality industry, and when it is high, founding a hotel chain is more attractive.

Aggregate Chain Units. As noted in chapter 7, there are two interpretations for Aggregate Chain Units: as a measure of a resource critical to chains, or as a proxy of competition in the chain population. Again, I think this variable should be seen as a measure of a resource (although the mortality analysis did not support this), and I predict a positive coefficient for Aggregate Chain Units.

Independent Hotels. The founding rate of chains should be negatively related to the size of this competing population. Independent Hotels should have a negative coefficient.

Aggregate Franchise Units. Supply of capital and the availability of organizational blue prints make it easier to found a hotel chain. This

Table 8–1
Correlations of Variables in
Founding Analysis

	(1)	(2)	(3)	(4)	(5)	(6)	(7)	(8)
(1) Density	1.0	.94	.62	-.04	.82	.83	.90	-.91
(2) Density²		1.0	.83	-.20	.77	.93	.73	-.83
(3) Franchise Units			1.0	-.12	.50	.90	.36	-.49
(4) Occupancy				1.0	-.31	-.22	-.23	.05
(5) Independent Hotels					1.0	-78	.73	-.90
(6) Chain Units						1.0	.63	-.76
(7) Log(Professional Managers)							1.0	-.80
(8) Agency Cost								1.0

suggests a positive coefficient for the effect of Aggregate Franchise Units on founding.

Table 8-1 shows the correlation matrix for these variables.

METHOD

The dependent variable here is a count of chain foundings in a discrete period (a year). Dependent variables of this type are referred to as event counts. Methods for the time-series analysis of continuous dependent variables are typically not adequate for analyzing event counts for two reasons (Amburgey and Carroll 1984). First, the models estimated will often predict fractional or negative counts. Second, standard time-series methods are not always the most efficient in a purely technical sense.

The Poisson model has been suggested as a basic approach to event counts (Amburgey and Carroll 1984; Cameron and Trivedi 1986; King 1988). To develop this model, let Y_i denote the number of occurrences, for the ith of N individuals of an event of interest in a given interval of time, $Y_i = 0,1,2 \ldots$ Let $y(t,\ t + \mathrm{d}t)$ denote the number of events observed in the interval $(t,\ t + \mathrm{d}t)$. Let λ_i be the mean and variance of Y_i. For the event-generating process to be a Poisson process of rate λ_i, the following set of assumptions must be satisfied:

(a) each unit in the sample has an equal probability of experiencing an event;
(b) the probability of an event occurring is constant over time;
(c) the probability of an event in the interval $(t,\ t + \mathrm{d}t)$ is independent of the history of the process up to time t; and
(d) the probability of two or more events occurring simultaneously is negligible.

If they are, the number of events in an interval of a given length is Poisson distributed with the probability density:

$$Pr(Y_i = y_i) = \frac{e^{-\lambda_i}\lambda_i^{y_i}}{y_i!}, \quad y_i = 0,1,2,\ldots, \quad i = 1,2,\ldots,N \qquad (8\text{–}1)$$

where y_i is the realized value of the random variable. To incorporate exogenous variables $X_{ij}(j = 1,...,K)$, including a constant, the parameter λ_i is specified to be:

$$\lambda_i = \exp(\boldsymbol{X}_i\beta) \, . \qquad (8\text{–}2)$$

In practice, the assumption that the conditional mean and variance of Y_i given X_i are equal is often violated. For reasons such as heteroscadasticity or contagion, the variance often exceeds the mean, a condition called overdispersion (Barron 1992). Overdispersion may produce spuriously small estimated standard errors of β(est), invalidating hypothesis testing. I tested for overdispersion using regression based techniques suggested by Cameron and Trivedi (1990). I also estimated two types of negative binomial models, which are used in the presence of overdispersion, described by Cameron and Trivedi (1986). The two models were the model they call NEGBIN I which assumes a constant ratio between the mean and the variance, and NEGBIN II which assumes a variance-mean ratio that is linear in the mean. After estimating these models I tested for the significance of the overdispersion parameters. These tests caused me to conclude that overdispersion was not present, and that Poisson regression was appropriate. Maximum-likelihood estimates were obtained using the statistical package LIMDEP (Greene 1992).

RESULTS

Table 8–2 shows three nested Poisson regressions. As with mortality, the first model includes traditional organizational ecology variables, the second adds environmental controls, and the third model adds variables that test hypotheses. As Table 8–3 shows, each model improves on the previous one, so the full model, Model 3, is discussed below.

Density (0.009, $p < .05$) and Density^2 (-.0001, $p < .01$) are significant in the directions predicted by the theory of density dependence. Further, all environmental controls are significant in the directions predicted above. The founding rate increases with Franchise Units (0.003, $p < .01$), Occupancy (0.02, $p < .01$) and Chain Units (0.00014, $p < .05$). The coefficient of Independent Hotels is negative and significant (-.017, $p < .01$), so consistent with the Lotka-Volterra competition equations, as the size of a competing population increases, the founding rate for chains decreases.

The hypotheses regarding the effects of environmental manipulations are also supported. The founding rate increases with Log(Professional

Table 8–2
Poisson Models of Hotel Chain Foundings, 1896–1980

Variable	(1)	(2)	(3)
Constant	0.935 **	-.31	2.12 *
	(.11)	(.43)	(1.1)
Density	0.013 **	0.03 **	0.009 *
	(.001)	(.003)	(.005)
Density^2	-.00002 **	-.0001 **	-.0001 **
	(.4E-05)	(.0000)	(.000)
Aggregate Franchise Units	—	0.003 **	0.003 **
		(.001)	(.001)
Occupancy	—	0.016 **	0.02 **
		(.005)	(.01)
Independent Hotels (1000'S)	—	-.008 *	-.017 **
		(.004)	(.01)
Aggregate Chain Units	—	0.0002 **	0.00014*
		(.000)	(.0001)
Log(Professional Managers)		—	0.236 **
			(.05)
Agency Cost	—	—	-.0098 **
			(.003)
Log-Likelihood	-284.6	-232.9	-218.6
Observations	85	85	85

One-tailed test of significance: + < .10, * < .05, ** < .01

Table 8–3
Comparison of Nested Poisson Regression Models from Table 8–2

Model	Added Variables	Log-likelihood	Log-likelihood Ratio of Comparison to Previous Model	Significance of Chi-Squared Test
(0)	Restricted-Slopes (1)	-492.89	—	—
(1)	Organizational Ecology (2)	-284.6	416.58	< .001
(2)	Environmental Controls (4)	-232.9	103.4	< .001
(3)	Hypotheses Testing (2)	-218.6	28.6	< .001

Managers), (0.236, $p < .01$), supporting hypothesis 4. The founding rate decreases with Agency Cost (-0.0098, $p < .01$). As hypothesis 6 suggests, as Agency Cost falls due to improvements in control systems, the founding rate of chains increases.

ISSUES AND REFINEMENTS OF THE FOUNDING ANALYSIS

The same problems that were raised in the mortality analysis (except unobserved heterogeneity) apply to the founding analysis. Because of the similarity between the problems and responses, I'll keep this discussion brief and refer the reader to chapter 7 for details.

I do not suspect a problem of multicolinearity because of the reasonably low correlations (Table 8–1) and the stable coefficients of models in Table 8–2 and other models not shown. As with the mortality rate, Figure 8–1 shows that there is high variability in the founding rate, so the high discrimination between a number of time-series is not surprising. The arguments against spurious correlation are also the same ones described in chapter 7: I hypothesized about the trends in the variables of substantive interest, and the models show (predicted) effects in opposite directions of variables with the same trend (such as Independent Hotels and Log(Professional Managers)). Further, neither Log(Professional Managers), Agency Cost, or the founding rate is monotonic.

As in the mortality analysis, I estimated a model with a five-year lag of the occupancy rate to address the possibility that the supply of professional managers responds to the fortunes of chains, rather than being "manipulated" by chain entrepreneurs and increasing the founding rate. Table 8–4 shows a comparison between Model 3 and alternative estimations. For ease of presentation, only the coefficients for variables of substantive interest are shown, although all control variables from the full model are used in the alternative estimations. Model 4 includes Lag(Occupancy). The variable is insignificant, and Model 4 does not improve over Model 3 ($\chi^2_{1df} = .6$, $p \approx .4$). A lag of munificence for the chain population does not improve the models, supporting my argument that the supply of professional managers drives chain foundings rather than simply responding to the success of chains.

I also tested the stock of Cornell graduates as an alternative operationalization of professional management. Model 5 is the full model using the stock instead of the flow of Cornell graduates. Log(Professional Managers) is still significant in the predicted direction (0.178, $p < .01$) so

Table 8–4
Alternate Estimations of Hotel Chain Foundings, 1896–1980

Variable	Full Model (4)	5 Year Lag of Occupancy (5)	Stock of Professional Managers (6)
Coefficients of Control Variables Are Not Shown			
Log(Professional Managers)	0.236 ** (.05)	0.238 ** (.05)	—
Agency Cost	-.0098 ** (.003)	-.011 ** (.003)	-.0128 ** (.003)
Lag(Occupancy)	—	-.003 (.003)	—
Log(Stock Professional Managers)	—	—	0.178 ** (.06)
Log-Likelihood	-218.6	-218.3	-223.2
Observations	85	85	85

One-tailed test of significance: + < .10, * < .05, ** < .01

hypothesis 4 is supported with both operationalizations. However, the fit of the model using stock appears worse than the model using flow (χ^2: -223.2 in Model 5 to -218.6 in Model 3). Further the significance of a number of the control variables is less in Model 5. Therefore, the flow operationalization is preferred as it was in the mortality analysis.

DISCUSSION OF FOUNDING RESULTS

The arguments about the effects of environmental manipulations received further support in the founding analysis. Founding rates increased because of the increases in the supply of professional managers and decreases in agency cost that chain entrepreneurs enacted. The founding models are further satisfying because all of the control variables were significant in the predicted directions.

Like the mortality models, the founding models are multiplicative. Coefficients cannot be interpreted in isolation, but multipliers of the ceteris-paribus rate can be calculated. I won't present graphs of the multiplier of the rate as I did for mortality, but I will describe the magnitude of the change. The multiplier of the rate for Log(Professional Managers) was 0.58 in 1896 and 3.61 in 1980. Holding all else constant, the founding rate increased more than 600% due to increases in the supply of professional managers. The multiplier of the rate for Agency Cost was 0.135 in 1896, and 0.788 in 1980, for an increase of almost 600%. Overall, the rate in 1980 was about 36 times the rate in 1896 due to these two environmental manipulations.

For the control variables, there is some disagreement between the implications of the founding and failure models. The non-monotonic effect of density is as predicted by the theory of density dependence. This is a little surprising because density had a monotonic effect on failure. As I explained in the last chapter, there is a possibility that the estimate of the effect of density on the failure rate was affected by multicolinearity. It may also be that legitimacy and competition work in different ways for founding and failure in this population. Also surprising considering the failure results is the coefficient for Aggregate Chain Units, the mass variable. In the failure model the positive coefficient for mass indicated increased competition with increases in the average size of chains, but in the founding model the positive coefficient for mass indicates an increased likelihood of new foundings as the average size of chains increases, which is not consistent with competition. Such differential influences of a variable on the founding and failure rate are unusual, but not unbelievable. Things that make it easy to found an organization do not necessarily make it easy for the organization to survive. Yet another difference between the implications of the founding and failure models is for independent hotels, for which the founding model showed inter-population competition, but the failure model did not.

The positive coefficient for Aggregate Franchise Units further supports the idea that franchising was important to the rise of hotel chains. The increased likelihood of foundings when there are more franchised hotels is consistent with the idea that one reason that franchising became popular in the hospitality industry despite the fact that it increases the failure rate of individual chains is that it helps unexperienced entrepreneurs found hotel chains.

9

Growth and Decline of Hotel Chains

When discussing the efficiency advantages and environmental manipulations that are the focus of this study, I hypothesized about effects on hotel chain foundings and failures, but not on hotel chain size. There are two reasons for this. First, the influences on organizational size have not been studied with anywhere near the rigor that organizational foundings and failures have been. A review on organizational growth and decline processes (Whetten 1987) cites almost no empirical studies of the causes of growth and decline. Because there has been so little past research on this topic, hypotheses development is hindered by a lack of understanding of basic processes. Second, the relationships between my variables of interest and size are complicated, and expectations are not clear. For example, consider the supply of professional managers. The argument most consistent with my claim that the supply of professional managers was critical to the rise of hotel chains would be that chain size would increase as professional managers increase. However, there are economies of scale with regard to executives: as an organization grows larger, the percentage of all employees who are top executives decreases (Daft and Becker 1978). So, it is at least feasible that chains might grow in response to a *shortage* of executives. Similarly, control systems may make large chains easier to operate, but it could be the case that advances in control systems made them useful for smaller chains.

Despite the difficulty in developing hypotheses, a study of chain size is vital to my arguments. I have demonstrated that changes in the institutional and technical environments made hotel chains more common, and that chains have certain efficiency advantages that increase their survival chances. But, if these same influences decreased the *size* of chains then my arguments may ultimately say nothing about the dominance of the chain form of organization. It could be the case that the variables I studied made chains more common, but also made them smaller. So, chain size must be studied

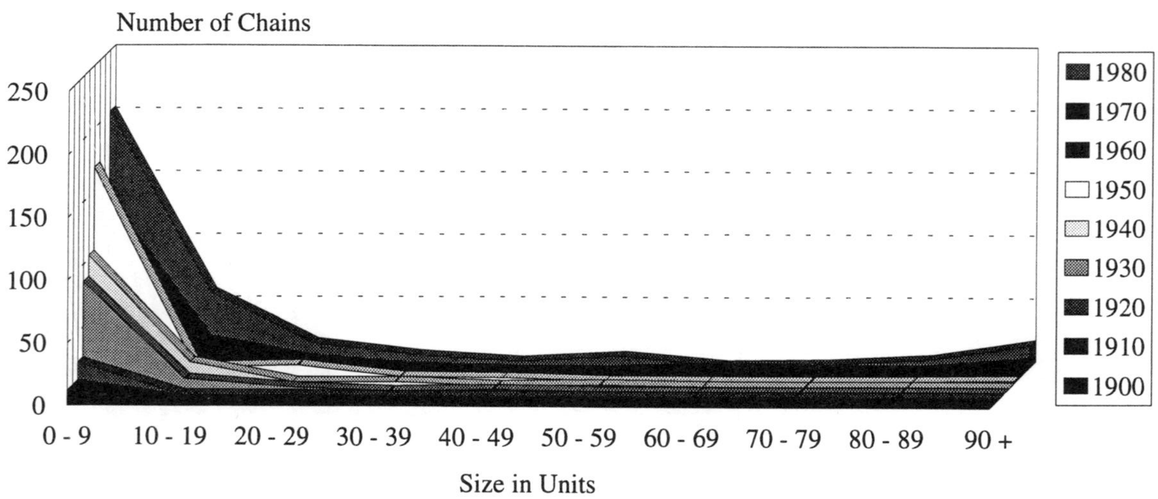

Figure 9-1. Size Distributions of Hotel Chains.

to make sure that size does not decrease with the supply of professional managers, the proliferation of control systems, and the opportunity for repeated interactions with customers. Further, the past neglect of organizational size as a subject of research makes it important to investigate it. The growth and decline of organizational forms is affected not only by changes in the numbers of organizations, but also by changes in their size. Any findings about what causes organizations to change in size are steps towards a more complete organizational ecology.

Figure 9–1 shows the size distributions for hotel chains at every ten year interval from 1900 to 1980. The figure indicates that larger chains became more common in later years. Until the 1970s, there were very few chains as large as ninety units. Table 9–1 lists the variables used in this analysis. An interesting variable that is absent from the list is the total franchise units. This variable was not included in the analysis because it caused multicolinearity. A brief description of my expectations for each variable follows.

Variables of Substantive Interest

Log(Professional Managers). Chapter 4 described professional managers as a necessary resource for chain operation. Chain size should be positively related to the supply of professional managers.

Agency Cost. Chapter 5 discussed agency cost as a problem for chains. Because of the separation of ownership and management, it is a problem that increases as size increases. There should be a negative relationship between chain size and Agency Cost.

Name Concentration. Chapter 3 described the advantages through repeated interaction that chains experience if they name their hotels consistently. There should be a positive relationship between chain size and Name Concentration.

City Concentration. Chapter 3 suggests chains with high concentration in one city will be better able to reap economies of scale. However, they will also have fewer opportunities to grow. Because of these contradicting influences, I have no expectation for the relationship between chain size and City Concentration.

Population-level Control Variables

Aggregate Chain Units. As described in previous chapters, the number of chain hotels can be considered as a resource for hotel chains. Controlling for

Table 9–1
Variables for Chain Size Analysis

Variable	Prediction	Description
Size	+	Dependent Variable. Number of hotels or motels in the chain.
Aggregate Chain $Units_t$	-	total hotels that are part of chains in a year.
Independent $Hotels_t$	-	total independent hotels in a year.
$Density_t$	+	total chains in a year.
Occupancy $Rate_t$	-	industry wide occupancy rate for the year.
$Log(Age)_{i,t}$	+	natural log of the chain's age.
$Regions_{i,t}$	+	the number of regions the chain operates in.
Log(Professional $Managers)_t$	-	natural log of the number of graduates from Cornell's hotel administration program for the year.
Agency $Cost_t$	+	general industry fidelity bonding rate.
Name $Concentration_{i,t}$	?	% of hotels in the chain with the name that is most common in the chain.
City $Concentration_{i,t}$		% of hotels in the chain in the city where the chain has the strongest presence.

all else, the size of hotel chains should be positively related to the number of chain units.

Independent Hotels. Independent hotels are the population of organizations that most closely competes with hotel chains. There should be a negative relationship between hotel chain size and the number of independent hotels.

Density. The number of hotel chains is a measure of the competition for resources, including chain hotels. Chain size should be negatively related to density.

Occupancy Rate. Occupancy rate summarizes the economic influences on the health of the hospitality industry. Chain size should be positively related to the occupancy rate.

Chain-Level Control Variables

Log(Age). As discussed in chapter 7, there is disagreement about the effect of age on organizations. My arguments that age creates inertia imply that organizations should become antiquated as they age. This suggests a negative relationship between a chain's size and its age. A number of recent papers have found that the rate of growth of organizations decreases with their age (Barron, West and Hannan 1994; Barnett 1994).

Regions. Chains in many geographic regions will have more opportunity for growth. Also, chains in many regions can reduce transportation expense per hotel by increasing in size. Finally, it has been suggested that one cause of organizational growth is to diversify risk (Whetten 1987). All these arguments suggest a positive relationship between a chain's size and the number of regions the chain operates in.

METHOD

Whetten (1987) notes that a critical failing of past research into organizational size has been a failure to model size dynamically. The goal of this analysis is to determine what causes hotel chains to grow larger, or decrease in size. Theoretically, the dependent variable of interest is the rate of change in the size of hotel chains. Coleman (1968) and Tuma and Hannan (1984) describe the partial-adjustment model for dynamic analysis. This model has been used by Haveman (1993b) to study the investment of savings and loan organizations in non-traditional markets, and by Freeman and Hannan (1975) to study the dynamics of organizational growth and decline. The partial-adjustment model is:

$$\frac{dy_t}{dt} = r[y_t^* - y_t] + \sigma Z_t \qquad (9\text{–}1)$$

where y_t is the actual size of the chain at time t; y^*_t is the target size for a chain with given characteristics in a given environment (the size towards which causal forces are moving the chain); r is the speed of adjustment toward this target; and σZ_t is a disturbance driven by white noise. y^*_t is assumed to depend linearly on organizational and environmental variables:

$$y_t^* = \beta X_t , \qquad (9\text{–}2)$$

where X_t is a vector of time varying organizational and environmental variables and β is a vector of coefficients. Substituting (9–2) into (9–1) yields:

$$\frac{dy_t}{dt} = r[\beta X_t - y_t] + \sigma Z_t . \qquad (9\text{–}3)$$

Equation 9-3 is referred to as the stochastic differential equation (SDE). The SDE cannot be estimated because the dependent variable is an instantaneous rate of change, and not observable. However, by assuming that the causal variables change linearly between observations (the validity of this assumption will be discussed), equation 9–3 can be integrated. The integral equation (IE) is:

$$y_t = \gamma y_{t-1} + \beta_1 x_{t-1} + \beta_2 \Delta x_{(t-1,t)} + \varepsilon_t , \qquad (9\text{–}4)$$

where y_t is the size of the chain in units; y_{t-1} is the lagged size of the chain (here the lag is five years); x_{t-1} is a vector of lags of the explanatory variables; and $\Delta x_{(t-1,t)}$ is a vector of changes in the explanatory variables during the period. The IE was estimated on the hotel chains observed at five year intervals.

The estimated parameters of the IE are related to those of the SDE as follows (Tuma and Hannan 1984, 341–344):

$$r = -\frac{\log[\gamma]}{\Delta t} , \qquad (9\text{–}5)$$

$$\beta \approx \frac{\beta_1 r}{\gamma - 1}, \qquad (9\text{–}6)$$

$$\beta \approx \frac{\beta_2 r^2}{\gamma - 1 - \log[\gamma]}, \qquad (9\text{–}7)$$

where Δt is the period between observations, five years. The two estimates of β have the same asymptotic expected value. As suggested by Tuma and Hannan (1984) the two estimates were averaged to calculate the coefficients reported here.

While point estimates of β can be obtained relatively easily, it is more difficult to obtain estimates of standard errors. Others who have used this model have not estimated standard errors for β, relying instead on statistical tests done on the IE to provide some evidence about the stability of estimates of β (Boeker 1991; Haveman 1993b). In doing so they assume that the ratios of standard errors to estimates of the IE to those of the SDE are the same, an assumption that is almost certainly false (Tuma and Hannan 1984). However, the covariance matrix of coefficients of the standard differential equation can be found by multiplying the transpose of the Jacobian matrix (J')of the function $f(\gamma, \beta_1, \beta_2)$ by that function's covariance matrix and multiplying the result by J. This procedure was performed to obtain estimates for the standard errors in the SDE.

POOLED TIME SERIES REGRESSION

The IE is estimable by OLS, but there are a number of challenges to the assumptions of OLS. The data set is a pooled time series as it contains a number of observations, T_i, for each of N hotel chains. The assumption of independence may be violated because multiple observations are linked with each chain. Further, the time-series and cross-sectional characteristics of the data raise risks of both autocorrelation and heteroscedasticity. These problems and the responses to them made here are discussed below.

Unit Effects

If there is heterogeneity across cross-sectional units a model of the basic form:

$$y_{it} = \alpha_i + \beta_1' x_{i,t-1} + \beta_2' \Delta x_{i,t-1,t} + \gamma y_{i,t-1} + \varepsilon_{it}, \qquad (9–8)$$

is appropriate (Greene 1990, 481). The individual effect is α_i, which is taken to be constant over time, t, and specific to the individual hotel chain, i. If the α_i's were the same across chains, OLS would provide consistent and efficient estimates of α, β_1, β_2, and γ. However, it seems likely that there should be chain-specific effects.

There are two methods of estimating equation (9–8) that allow for chain specific effects. The first is the fixed-effects model, which estimates α_i for every chain. This procedure is costly as a degree of freedom is lost for each cross-sectional unit (in this case there are more than 400 chains). An alternative is the random-effects model which treats the individual-specific constant terms as randomly distributed across cross-sectional units. Because I am not interested in chain-specific effects, and because the fixed-effects model costs about one third of the degrees of freedom, I prefer the random-effects model for this analysis. However, the random-effects model uses a questionable assumption that should be tested before proceeding. It assumes that the individual effects are uncorrelated with the other regressors. Hausman offers a test (described in Greene 1990, 495) of this assumption based on the idea that under the hypothesis of no correlation, both the fixed-effects and random-effects models are consistent, but under the alternative fixed-effects is consistent, but random-effects is not. This test was performed and the hypothesis of no correlation was not rejected. This supports the use random-effects model. A test of the random-effects model against OLS without chain-specific events also supported the random-effects model. Therefore, the random effects model was used for the analysis. The reformulation of (9–8) is:

$$y_{it} = \beta_1' x_{i,t-1} + \beta_2' \Delta x_{i,t-1,t} + \gamma y_{i,t-1} + u_i + \varepsilon_{it}, \qquad (9–9)$$

where u_i is the random disturbance characterizing the ith observation and is constant through time. Greene (1990, 486) lists the assumptions for the errors. This model was estimated with a GLS regression described by Greene (1990, 487–488). The variance of the combined disturbance terms was estimated using the means method (Greene 1990, 490).

Autocorrelation

Autocorrelation, or serial correlation of disturbances across periods, is a common problem in time-series analysis. Typically, autocorrelation causes least squares to be inefficient, although unbiased and consistent. However, if the regressions include lagged values of the dependent variable, as the ones estimated here do, least squares is no longer unbiased or consistent. This makes it more important to correct for autocorrelation, and more difficult to detect and estimate it.

The Durbin-Watson statistic is most frequently used as a test for autocorrelation, but it is unlikely to be valid in the presence of a lagged dependent variable (Greene 1990, 454). Instead I used a modification of the Breusch-Godfrey test suggested by Durbin, and referred to as the *m* test by Kmenta (1986, 333). In this test e_t is regressed on x_t, y_{t-1}, and e_{t-1}. Since X'e = 0, the test is equivalent to regressing e_t on the part of the lagged residuals that is unexplained by X. If any fit is found it is due to the correlation between the current and lagged residuals. A significant fit was found, indicating first order autocorrelation.

Correcting for autocorrelation involves a two step *Estimated Generalized Least Squares* (EGLS) approach (Ostrom 1990). This involves estimating the parameters of the autocorrelative process, then transforming the data and applying OLS. I seek to estimate a model of the form:

$$y_{it} = \beta_1' x_{i,t-1} + \beta_2' \Delta x_{i,t-1,t} + \gamma y_{i,t-1} + \varepsilon_{it} + u_i \,, \qquad (9\text{–}10)$$

$$\varepsilon_{it} = \rho \varepsilon_{i,t-1} + \eta_{it} \,. \qquad (9\text{–}11)$$

Note that the autocorrelation is embodied in the unique component. First, the autocorrelation coefficient, ρ, must be estimated. When a model contains a lagged dependent variable OLS does not yield accurate estimates of the error term, and therefore does not provide consistent estimates of autocorrelation. The instrumental variables technique can be used in this circumstance (Greene 1990; Ostrom 1990). This involves estimating the lagged dependent variable using variables that are not correlated with the error term. Greene (1990, 448) suggests that the fitted values in the regression of y_t on x_t and x_{t-1} can be used as estimates of y_{t-1}. The errors from a regression of y_t on x_t, x_{t-1} and the estimate of y_{t-1} are consistent, and were used to estimate ρ.

With the estimate of ρ, the second step of EGLS is possible. The data were transformed as follows:

$$Z_1^* = (1-\rho^2)^{.5} Z_1 \qquad (9\text{–}12)$$

$$Z_t^* = Z_t - \rho Z_{t-1} \quad (t > 1)\,, \qquad (9\text{–}13)$$

where Z is used for Y and X, and t represents observations 2,3, . . . n for each chain's time series. This transformation is preferable to the Cochrane-Orcutt technique because it preserves the first estimate for each time series, and yields more accurate estimates when each time series is short (Green 1990, 443, Haveman 1993b). The transformed data was used in the OLS estimation.

Heteroscedasticity

When the variance in the error term of the estimated model is not consistent across observations (when the error term is not homoscedastic), then OLS estimates are no longer "best" or "efficient"; the variances of coefficients are biased upwards. Heteroscedasticity often occurs because errors vary with some measure of the size of the observation. Large observations may be associated with greater variance in the error. The Goldfeld-Quandt test for heteroscedasticity was applied here. This test involves ordering the data by the variable suspected of causing heteroscedasticity, in this case lagged size, dividing the sample into two groups, estimating the regression separately on each set of observations, and comparing the disturbance variances. Under the assumption of homoscedasticity, the disturbance variances would be the same in both groups, while under the alternative, the disturbance variances would differ. This test indicated the presence of heteroscedasticity.

Heteroscedasticity can be adjusted for by weighing each variable in the regression by the proportionality variable (Greene 1990). Here, the square-root of lagged size was used to weight the variables.

Table 9–2

Integral Equation Estimates and Transformations to Stochastic Differential Equation, Hotel Chain Size, 1896-1980

Estimation of Integral Equation			Transformation to Stochastic Differential Equation		
Variable	Coefficient	S.E.	Variable	Coefficient	S.E.
Chain Size$_{t-1}$	0.9125 **	(0.0043)	Rate of Adjustment	0.0183 **	(0.0001)
Agg. Chain Units$_{t-1}$	0.0163 **	(0.0060)	Aggregate Chain Units	0.0026	(0.0028)
Independent Hotels$_{t-1}$	-.8200 *	(0.3189)	Independent Hotels	-.0604	(0.1213)
Density$_{t-1}$	-1.713 **	(0.3622)	Density	-.2122 *	(0.0934)
Occupancy Rate$_{t-1}$	3.0271 **	(0.6867)	Occupancy Rate	0.3751 *	(0.1888)
Log(Age)$_{t-1}$	-15.64 **	(2.1510)	Log(Age)	-2.529 **	(0.8196)
Regions$_{t-1}$	13.417 **	(0.5722)	Regions	1.7889 **	(0.1670)
Log(Managers)$_{t-1}$	33.885 **	(5.9740)	Log(Professional Managers)	3.9018 **	(1.0607)
Agency Cost$_{t-1}$	-.8521 **	(0.1565)	Agency Cost	-.1040 **	(0.0182)
Name Concent.$_{t-1}$	51.320 **	(3.9380)	Name Concentration	6.3705 **	(1.1263)
City Concent.$_{t-1}$	17.235 **	(4.4240)	City Concentration	2.1962	(1.3671)
ΔAgg. Chain Units	0.0220 *	(0.0104)			
ΔIndependent Hotels	0.6126	(0.7300)			
ΔDensity	-.7976 **	(0.2727)			
ΔOccupancy Rate	1.4164 *	(0.5799)			
ΔLog(Age)	-21.66 **	(2.9020)			
ΔRegions	9.3332 **	(0.6210)			
ΔLog(Managers)	8.6311 **	(2.4370)			
ΔAgency Cost	-.3590 **	(0.0671)			
ΔName Concent.	24.265 **	(4.1650)			
ΔCity Concent.	9.5220 *	(5.1920)			

Significance (two-tailed test): + < .10, * < .05, ** < .01

RESULTS

There were 1241 observations after considering each five-year span of a chain's history. Table 9–2 shows the results of the estimation of the IE, and the transformed coefficients and standard errors of the SDE. Because formal hypotheses were not developed, two-tailed tests were used to determine the significance of the SDE coefficients.

The rate of adjustment of the SDE, (r in equation 9–3) is .0183. This indicates that chains close about 2% of the gap between their target size and their current size each year. This is surprisingly low. It indicates that inertia dominates the size of hotel chains. The finding is intriguing because hotel chains seem to be relatively easy organizations to grow or shrink because units can simply be purchased or sold. If analyses similar to this one were conducted for other types of organizations, it would be interesting to compare the rates of adjustment.

Among the population-level control variables, Aggregate Chain Units and the number of Independent Hotels were not significant. However, a measurement problem may have been responsible for the non-significance of Independent Hotels. The number of independent hotels was obtained from census publications, and is known only at irregular intervals. Indeed, the IE estimates of this variable had signs in opposite directions, suggesting a violation of the assumption of linear change of the variable between observations.

The other two population-level control variables were significant in the expected directions. Density was negative and significant (-0.2122, $p < .05$) indicating that the equilibrium size of chains decreases as the number of chains increases. This is evidence that competition increases with density, and is consistent with results from the founding and failure analyses. Occupancy was positive and significant (0.3751, $p < .05$). As expected, the equilibrium size of chains increases with this catch-all index of the strength of the hospitality industry.

Turning to the chain-level controls, Log(Age) was negative and significant (-2.529, $p < .01$). This supports the expectation suggested by the argument that inertia increases with age. This is a compelling result, especially in light of the contradicting views about the effects of age on organizations.

The other chain-level control, Regions, was positive and significant (1.789, $p < .01$). As expected, regionally dispersed chains have a larger equilibrium size. These chains have more opportunities for growth, and are more able to pursue a strategy of risk diversification.

The variables of primary interest to this study were significant in the expected directions. Log(Professional Managers) was significant and positive (3.9018, $p < .01$). As the supply of professional managers increased, the equilibrium size of hotel chains also increased. This supports the argument that professional managers were a critical resource facilitating the growth of hotel chains. Agency Cost was significant and negative (-.1040, $p < .01$). This suggests that when agency costs were high, before the control revolution in hotel chains, the equilibrium size of hotel chains was smaller than in the post-control revolution period. Because the coefficients represent linear effects on the equilibrium size of chains it is easy to determine the magnitude of the effect of these environmental manipulations. Table 9–3 shows that these environmental manipulations resulted in significant increases in the equilibrium size of hotel chains.

Name Concentration was significant and positive (6.37, $p < .01$). This supports the repeated interaction argument made in chapter 3. This is particularly satisfying because the dynamic nature of this analysis helps to dismiss alternative explanations for the effect of Name Concentration (see below). City Concentration, for which I had no expectation, was not significant.

Table 9–3
Effects of Environmental Manipulations on Chain Size

Variable	Δ from 1896 to 1980	Coefficient from Table 9–2	Effect on Size (In units)
Log (Professional Managers)	7.71	3.9018	30.08
Agency Cost	-173.78	-.1040	18.07

DISCUSSION

The results of the analysis of chain growth and decline are exciting for two reasons. First, they support the theoretical arguments and the findings of the mortality and founding studies. The unique contribution of this work has been the argument that the hotel chain form developed partly because of strategic manipulation of the environment by hotel chain entrepreneurs. It would have been a serious challenge to that argument if chain size had been found to decrease with changes in agency costs and the supply of professional managers. However, chain size was found to increase with these changes. The analysis also supports the argument that one of the advantages of the chain form was an ability to engage in repeated interactions and build reputations.

Further, this analysis contributes to arguments I have made about the causal underpinnings of results of the mortality and founding studies. Both of those studies use dynamic methods. They are both longitudinal, and both focus on marginal changes in the number of hotel chains (deaths and births). However, I have noted that there are reasonable arguments that challenge the causal implications I draw from those studies. Specifically, it is possible that the number of professional managers increases in response to increases in foundings and decreases in mortality of hotel chains. It is also possible that hotel chains follow different naming strategies because of differences in the hotels they own. I have presented evidence to refute both of those possibilities. However, the findings here are perhaps the best refutations I can offer. In this analysis, the effect of changes in the independent variables was *explicitly modeled*. The increase or decrease in professional managers, and in the name concentration of chains were included in models, and contributed to estimations of the effect of professional managers and name concentration on size. While founding (mortality) models showed that foundings (deaths) were high when professional managers were abundant (scarce), these models demonstrate that size increased when the supply of professional managers increased.

Second, the dynamics of size is a neglected area of organizational theory. This analysis suggests a number of fertile topics for future study. Generally, the results here demonstrate that organizations do not only begin and end in response to their environments, they also grow and shrink. The relationship between density and size is consistent with other ecological arguments. The relationship between age and size provides fresh evidence for a controversy that has so far not been resolved in countless mortality studies. The findings that strategy, as expressed for instance by name concentration, effects size suggest yet another dependent variable for the strategy literature which has struggled for an operational definition of organizational performance. Evidence of the rate of adjustment provides a measure of the speed of change, which would be a basis for a fascinating comparison of the level of inertia in different populations of organizations.

10

Comparison to Independent Hotels

I introduced this book by describing the transition from independent to chain ownership of hotels in the U.S. Since then I have hypothesized that efficiency advantages and environmental manipulations have favored chains, and found evidence in support of my hypotheses. Implicit in that exercise is the idea that those things that favored chains did not favor independent hotels, or at least did not favor them as much, and therefore account at least partially for the increasing dominance of chains in the hospitality industry.

For the efficiency advantages of chains this implication is not problematic. Independent hotels are smaller than chains, and chains have greater likelihood of repeated interactions with customers. So if, as I have demonstrated, these things are advantages, they are advantages that chains have over independent hotels.

For the environmental manipulations that favor chains there is a challenge. I explained that I believe that these manipulations favor chains over independent hotels because independent hotels do not rely on professional managers, and do not suffer from agency problems as much as chains do. However, there are reasonable arguments to the contrary. For instance, it could be argued that professional managers are able to make independent hotels more efficient. It is at least conceivable that the environmental manipulations that benefitted chains benefitted independent hotels as well.

There are two reasons why my arguments would be threatened if the supply of professional managers and the increase in internal control helped all hotel organizations as much as chains. First, it would mean that the *transition* from independent to chain organization remains unexplained. I would still have valid evidence about the growth of the chain form, but not about the historical phenomenon that motivated my interest in the hospitality industry. The second threat to my arguments is probably more important. I have claimed that chain entrepreneurs manipulated the institutional and technical environments to favor their organizations and their organizational form. If those manipulations actually benefitted all hotel organizations then there was no motivation for chain entrepreneurs to go to the trouble of changing the environment. If the environmental changes actually benefitted the competitors of hotel chains as much as chains, then my argument about actors manipulating environments amounts to a claim that chain entrepreneurs went through a costly process that gave them no relative benefit.

In order to answer these challenges I will perform a test. In this chapter I examine the effects of the environmental manipulations on a population of independent hotels.

THE POPULATION OF INDEPENDENT HOTELS AT NIAGARA FALLS

The population I use for this test is the population of independent hotels at Niagara Falls. This data is described in detail in Ingram and Inman (1997). It includes independent hotels in the cities of Niagara Falls, New York and Niagara Falls, Ontario between 1890 and 1992. The principle sources of data were city directories and telephone books in those two cities. The life histories of 1,223 hotels covering 13,627 one year spells are included.

To test the effects of the environmental manipulations on independent hotels, I included the Log(Professional Managers) and Agency Cost variables in models of mortality and founding of independent hotels in Niagara Falls. Because it is not easy for a single hotel to change in size an analysis of growth and decline would be inappropriate. My expectation is that independent hotel mortality will be unaffected or increase, and independent hotel founding will be unaffected, or decrease with the changes in Log(Professional Managers) and Agency Cost.

I will not discuss the models in detail because it is only the effects of Log(Professional Managers) and Agency Cost that are of interest here. Readers who are interested in the many influences on founding and failure of Niagara Falls hotels should see Ingram and Inman (1997), which reports extensive analyses of these processes. In the models estimated to examine the effect of the environmental manipulations caused by chain entrepreneurs, I did include typical variables such as Density and Density-squared. I also controlled for some of the idiosyncracies of the Niagara Falls population by including a variable that captures the strength of the public parks at Niagara Falls, and "localized-competition" measures (Baum and Mezias 1992) that capture the fact that there are two sub-populations of hotels, one in each city. I used procedures similar to those described in chapters 7 and 8 to estimate failure and founding models of Niagara Falls hotels.

RESULTS AND DISCUSSION

Table 10–1 summarizes the results of the analyses on independent hotels and compares them to the results for chains. The effects in the table are the net effect of the environmental manipulation on the vital rate. For instance, Agency Cost was positively related to chain mortality and Agency Cost decreased historically so the net effect of the environmental manipulation is to decrease chain mortality.

As has been discussed, the environmental manipulations decreased the mortality rate and increased the founding rate of hotel chains. For independent hotels the environmental manipulations had no significant effect on the mortality rate. The founding rate of independent hotels decreased with the environmental manipulations. Therefore, this test supports my arguments that increases in the supply of professional managers and the sophistication of internal control helped hotel chains but not independent hotels. The effects of these environmental changes on vital rates caused chains to be more numerous and independent hotels to be less numerous.

It is possible that other populations of independent hotels would be affected differently than Niagara Falls hotels by increases in professional managers and decreases in agency cost. It is particularly likely that a population dominated by large independent hotels would be favored by the same environmental manipulations that favored hotel chains. Very large hotels, such as the ones that are common in Manhattan and Chicago, are in some ways more similar to hotel chains than to small independent hotels. Very large hotels need professional managers and internal control almost as much as hotel chains do. In fact, some big city hotels manage more rooms than some small chains.

Table 10–1
Comparison of Effect of Environmental Manipulations on
Vital Rates of Hotel Chains and Independent Hotels

Effects are not the sign of the coefficient from the statistical model, but rather the direction of the historic effect. For instance, the mortality of chains is positively related to Agency Cost, and Agency Cost decreases historically, so the historic effect is a decrease in the mortality rate of chains (-).

	Hotel Chains	Independent Hotels
Mortality Rate:		
Institutional Change; Supply of Professional Managers.	-	no significant effect
Technical Change; Decrease of Agency Cost	-	no significant effect
Founding Rate:		
Institutional Change; Supply of Professional Managers.	+	-
Technical Change; Decrease of Agency Cost	+	-

11

Discussion and Conclusion

The main arguments of this book, which were represented by hypotheses, were all supported. The results indicate first that there are strategic advantages associated with operating a hotel chain. There are economies of scale available for hotel chains. Larger, more concentrated chains are more robust. Also, the results show that hotel chains can use repeated interactions to solve the incentive problems that independent hotels face. Simply having more hotels with the same name increases the survival chances and growth rates of hotel chains.

The changes in the institutional environment caused by the entrepreneurs who led the early hotel chains benefitted the population. As the supply of professional managers to the hotel industry increased, mainly through university education supported by the industry, founding and growth rates of hotel chains increased and mortality rates decreased. Similarly, changes in the technical environment that were brought about by hotel chain entrepreneurs benefitted the population. Accounting and management information systems available to hotel chains improved throughout the twentieth century. These systems solved agency problems, increasing founding and growth rates and decreasing mortality rates.

These results, and other details from the analyses, are informative about the hotel industry. Hospitality is the third biggest industry in the U.S. by revenues, and deserves to be the subject of scholarly attention. One of the interesting implications of the results for the hospitality industry is the inconclusive findings concerning competition between chains and independent hotels. This competition may be most productively studied at the level of the individual hotel by examining competition between independent hotels and chain hotels. Competition among hotel chains is also an issue worthy of additional research. All three dynamic analyses performed here showed that hotel chains compete with each other, but it seems likely that there are subtleties to the competitive relationships of chains that were not revealed by the analyses. It is particularly likely that hotel chains engage in localized competition (Baum and Mezias 1992). Hotel chains are geographically distributed, and competition between them may depend on the extent to which they operate in the same regions or cities. The fact that two chains may compete with each other in more than one market is also a relevant issue as such multipoint relationships may affect the intensity of competitive rivalry.

Although I focused on two environmental changes that chain entrepreneurs were instrumental in, there were other environmental changes that were not in the control of hoteliers. Changes in transportation methods and travel patterns also affected the hotel industry. The growth of the interstate highway system occurred around the same time that motels and motel chains became more common (Belasco 1979). The first chains to grow very large, Holiday Inn and Howard Johnson's, had much of their initial growth along the main highways between Canada and Florida. To explain the spatial evolution of hotel chains, from state to state, changes in transportation and travel would have to be considered.

Franchising also appears to be an important environmental change in the hospitality industry. Founding rates increased and failure rates decreased as a function of the aggregate level of franchising. Franchising started relatively late in the period I examine in this book. The first hotel chains to be franchisees did not appear until 1960. Franchising grew quickly between 1960 and 1980, and has grown even more quickly since 1980. In fact, franchising might be characterized as representing a second era of environmental change, after the changes I examined, that is critical to the evolution of hotel chains since 1980. The effect of franchising on hotel chains is made more interesting because the chains that are directly involved in franchising suffer higher rates of failure.

The results on the rise of hotel chains may also be representative of more general processes. First, the rise of hotel chains may be a typical example of the rise of the chain form of organization in other industries. Second, the arguments made here about the interaction between actors with interests in certain organizations and the environment address important problems in organizational theory. They can contribute to our understanding of the creation of institutional and technical environments, and the role of entrepreneurship in the face of environmental constraint.

THE CHAIN FORM OF ORGANIZATION ACROSS INDUSTRIES

The changes in the form of organization in the hospitality industry are not unique. In fact, it seems that the chain form of organization will become common in every industry where there are transactions between the organization and the ultimate consumer. In the early twentieth century the chain form became dominant in all types of retail enterprises. During this century it grew in importance in industries such as food service, hospitality, insurance and banking. Now chains are even taking hold in industries that seemed unsusceptible to professional management, such as health care. Figure 11–1 shows the growth in the share of revenue earned by multi-unit organizations in a number of service industries.

The three parts of the argument I use to explain the rise of hotel chains can at least partly be applied to explain the rise of the chain form in other service industries. Below I discuss the generalizability of the efficiency advantages, institutional changes and technical changes of hotel chains to other industries.

Efficiency Advantages

Economies of scale (and scope) are idiosyncratic to industries. All industries probably have some economies of scale, but there is certainly variance in the importance of this advantage. Some organizations such as supermarkets and hospitals may realize significant efficiencies in the purchase of materials and the utilization of equipment and facilities by increasing in size. Most service organizations enjoy economies of scale for advertising and communications technology. A form of economies of scale may also derive from the fact that larger organizations generate more experience, for instance, in choosing good locations for stores (Lebhar 1959).

The repeated interaction advantage of hotel chains appears to have wide application to other industries. Fast food chains became the first choice of travelers because they were able to offer more consistency than independent restaurants (Belasco 1979). Auto repair chains can offer customers guarantees that will be honored across the country. In other industries, multi-unit operation does not necessarily raise the likelihood of repeated interaction, but it does increase the stake that the business has in satisfying the customer. Sears will do more to protect its reputation of customer service than a neighborhood appliance store because it profits much more from that reputation.

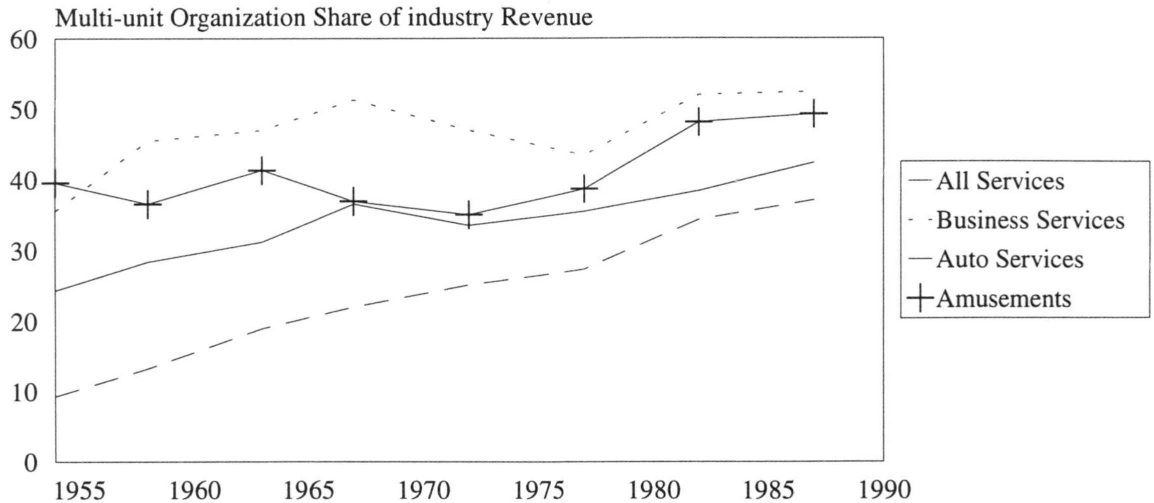

Figure 11-1. Revenue Shares of Multi-Unit Organizations in Selected Service Industries.
Source: U.S. Census of Business

The Supply of Professional Managers

Few industries have dedicated university programs to produce their managers as the hospitality industry does. However, general sources of professional managers, business schools, have flourished at a rate comparable to that of hotel schools. Between 1920 and 1958 the number of university degrees granted in business rose from 1,686 to 55,404 (Gordon and Howell 1959). It seems unlikely that interested entrepreneurs would have found it profitable to influence business schools as they did hotel schools. But, although the causes of business school growth may be different from the causes of hotel school growth, the effects on forms of organization may be similar. Professionally managed organizations of all types may be made more feasible by increases in the number of business school graduates.

The Control Revolution

One of the most striking features of business history since the industrial revolution has been the constant increases in the sophistication of technologies that control workers and work (Beniger 1986). Different industries, however, have different challenges to effective control. Service industries have particular agency problems because their systems cannot rely on the physical flow of easily measured goods. It is also more difficult to apply control technology to regulate the speed of work in service industries. Perhaps the lack of effective control technology has acted as a constraint on the diffusion of multi-unit organizations in service industries. Casual observation supports this claim. The first service industries to adopt the chain form were those such as retailing, where control is relatively easy. The service organizations that have held on to independent ownership the longest are professional organizations such as accounting firms and hospitals where control (both procedural and mechanized) is particularly difficult.

The increase in the supply of professional managers could also be characterized as an advance in control technology. In his book *The Control Revolution*, Beniger (1986) documents the many facets of progress in control. He describes some of the other environmental changes that may have facilitated the growth of the chain form of organization. Distribution, transportation and advertising were all revolutionized in ways that favored the chain. Some of these changes involved political battles of the kind that surrounded the environmental changes described in this study. For instance, independent retailers aggressively opposed chain stores, lobbying for special sales taxes and zoning laws to restrict chains. Most states eventually enacted some type of anti-chain-store legislation (341).

EXPLAINING ENVIRONMENTS

The idea that environmental conditions can and should be explained has important implications for two of the most currently influential organizational theories. As I pointed out in chapter 1, organizational ecology relies on the environment to explain organizational diversity. As long as the demands of the environment are treated as exogenous, accounts of the rise and fall of organizational forms will be incomplete. Similarly, institutional theorists have until now said little about the creation and change of institutions. If, as I have argued, institutions are affected by actors pursuing their interests, the "preconscious" mechanisms of many views of institutional influence must be reconsidered.

While the arguments I have made contribute to those established theories, I think they are sufficiently distinct as to suggest a (nearly) original approach. Various components of this study seem like typical institutional or ecological research. But when viewed in entirety it is clear that an important determinant of the success and failure of organizations in the hospitality industry was the outcome of intentional efforts to control the environment. The interests of actors and groups of actors, and the power they can muster in support of those interests ultimately cause certain organizational forms to be favored over others. Because power and interest are its critical explanatory tools, this position could be thought of as a political economy of organizations.

Consistent with the categorization of my approach as political economy, Alt and Shepsle (1990, 2) claim that the emerging "positive political economy" deals with two characteristic questions: "How do observed differences among institutions affect political and economic outcomes and how are institutions themselves affected by individual and collective beliefs, preferences and strategies?" Since the institutions of Alt and Shepsle coincide with the socially constructed elements of the organizational environment, I can paraphrase them to summarize my challenge to organizational theory: How do observed differences among environments affect organizational outcomes and how are environments themselves affected by individual and collective beliefs, preferences and strategies? The first question has been the focus of organizational theory for two decades. The second question has been occasionally touched on (by for example Zald 1970 and Pfeffer and Salancik 1978). I think the recognition that the questions must be considered together is a unique and compelling result of this study.

CONCLUSION

The rise of hotel chains is a defining phenomenon of one of the most important industries in the American economy. The analyses here demonstrate two strategic benefits of chains in the hotel industry. Chains enjoy economies of scale, and solve interaction problems between hotels and customers by creating the opportunity for repeated interaction. A century ago, it was difficult to take advantage of these strategic advantages by successfully operating a hotel chain because of the unavailability of professional managers, and the weakness of available internal control systems. Since 1896, the supply of professional managers to the hotel industry and the sophistication of control systems have increased. Chain entrepreneurs were instrumental in causing these changes in the operating environment faced by chains. As the environment changed in these two ways, chains were founded more, grew faster, and failed less.

The environment is important in many theories of why organizations look and act the way they do, but this powerful explanatory force is almost always taken as exogenous. In this study I note that environments must come from somewhere, and argue that actors affected by the environment are a good place to start a theory of the origin and change of environments. I have briefly described two campaigns where entrepreneurs manipulated the environment to favor the organizations they operated, or hoped to operate. This study only hints at the complexity of environmental manipulation. The process is political, involving coalitions of, and competition between interests. Predicting its outcome requires identifying the interests actors hold and the power they can muster. I hope that in this study I demonstrated that sometimes full explanations of organizational phenomena require that environments be seen as outcomes of interested action before they are used as independent variables.

NOTES

Chapter 3: Advantages of Hotel Chains

1. Traveling salesmen were an exception to this. However, it is consistent with the argument I am developing that there were hotels that catered specifically to traveling salesmen. Hotels were able to differentiate between customers for whom there was a large possibility of a future encounter and customers for whom there was not. Further, the time when chains began to replace independent hotels corresponded with a change in the way traveling salesmen did business. The automobile made it convenient for salesmen to cover larger territories, and to spend part of a day in town where previously they would have had to stay overnight. The success of catalogue shopping in the early twentieth century also reduced the importance of traveling salesmen (Hayner 1936, 38–39).

Even in their heyday, traveling salesmen were not always able to use the ability to withhold future patronage to get good service at hotels. They were most active in rural America. This meant that often they could not take advantage of past experience with a hotel, because in a small town where they had no relatives, they had no alternative to staying at the local hotel. Like the "one shot" travelers I analyze in detail, they attempted to increase the weight of their encounters with hotels, although they did so by banding together rather than by raising the shadow of the future. Salesmen's groups were instrumental in passing many laws demanding safety features in hotels. They also attempted to have the industry regulated as a monopoly, and threatened to establish their own hotel chain (AHMA Archives).

2. Actually the hotel moves first in this simple game because it chooses its level of service before the customer decides whether or not to stay at the hotel. However, since that move is unobservable to the customer the simultaneous-move game is appropriate.

Chapter 4: Institutional Change

1. One anonymous commentator characterized the problem of transient labor with this fictitious complaint made by a manager: "Yesterday I hired a highly recommended German chef who spoke English well and made a big hit with Irish dishes, but this morning he showed his American independence and took French leave" (AHMA Archives, III 50).

2. Probably the most divisive issue for associations of hoteliers in the first quarter of the twentieth century was the dominance of operators from the North East, mostly New York City. Westerners were most vocal about the lack of attention to their interests. Sam Dutton, a Colorado hotelier (trained in the Fred Harvey System) championed a "see America first" campaign that at times threatened to divide the AHA. Dutton and others felt that Eastern hoteliers ignored the necessity of promoting domestic travel. The rallying cry for Dutton's movement was "see Europe if you must, but see America first."

Ultimately, the only way the AHA was able to establish itself as a stable, national association was to adopt in 1921 the "Pellow Plan" (Robert Pellow was the San Antonio, TX hotelier who first proposed the plan). This reorganization gave increased voting privileges to state hotel associations. Eventually, the AHA (later the AHMA) would become a federation of state hotel associations.

Chapter 9: Growth and Decline of Hotel Chains

2. Sociological studies using partial-adjustment models move awkwardly between deterministic and stochastic representations. Stochastic versions of these models are very complicated. The typical response to this is to present a deterministic model, but to estimate it using statistical techniques, and to make back-handed inferences about parameters. However, if the disturbances are assumed to be driven by white noise, as they are here, a stochastic treatment is greatly simplified (Tuma and Hannan 1984). I make this assumption because of the benefits of a stochastic treatment but I must note that in this case (as in most sociological applications) the presence of a lower boundary to the dependent variable makes the assumption of white noise problematic.

REFERENCES

Alarm Clock. 1928. How they got away with it. Incident No. 21. *Alarm Clock*. (September 8):5.

Alexander, Jeffrey C., and Philip Smith. 1993. The discourse of American civil society: A new proposal for cultural studies. *Theory and Society* 22:151–208.

Alt, James E., and Kenneth A. Shepsle. 1990. Editors' introduction. In *Perspectives on positive political economy*, edited by J.E. Alt and K.A. Shepsle. New York: Cambridge University Press.

Amburgey, Terry L., and Glenn R. Carroll. 1984. Time-series models for even counts. *Social Science Research* 13:38–54.

Amburgey, Terry L., Dawn Kelly, and William P. Barnett. 1993. Resetting the clock: The dynamics of organizational change and failure. *Administrative Science Quarterly* 38:51–73.

American Hotel and Motel Association (AHMA). Archives. Washington, D.C.

American Hotel Association Directory Company. 1931 to 1981. *Directory of Hotel and Motel Systems*. Washington, D.C.:American Hotel Association Directory Company.

Anderson, Sherwood. 1947. *Winesburg, Ohio*. New York: Random House.

Astley, W. Graham, and Andrew H. Van de Ven. 1983. Central perspectives and debates in organizational theory. *Administrative Science Quarterly* 28: 243–273.

Barnett, William P. 1994. The liability of collective action: Growth and change among early American telephone companies. In *Evolutionary dynamics of organizations*, edited by J.A.C. Baum and J.V. Singh, 337–354. New York: Oxford.

Barnett, William P., and Terry L. Amburgey. 1990. Do larger organizations generate stronger competition? In *Organizational evolution: New directions*, edited by J.V. Singh, 78–102. Newbury Park, CA: Sage.

Barron, David N. 1992. The analysis of count data: Overdispersion and autocorrelation. *Sociological Methodology* 22: 179–220.

Barron, David N., Elizabeth West and Michael T. Hannan. 1994. A time to grow and a time to die: Growth and mortality of credit unions in New York, 1914–1990. *American Journal of Sociology* 100: 381–421.

Baum, Joel A.C. 1989. Liabilities of newness, adolescence, and obsolescence Exploring age dependence in the dissolution of organizational relationships and organizations. *Proceedings of the Administrative Sciences Association of Canada* 10(5):1–10.

———. 1996. Organizational Ecology. In *Handbook of organizational studies*, edited by S.R. Clegg, C. Hardy, and W. Nord, forthcoming. London: Sage.

Baum, Joel A. C. and Theresa K. Lant. 1993. Cognitive categorization of competitors and competitive intensity in the Manhattan hotel industry Paper presented at the Academy of Management meetings, August, Dallas, TX.

Baum, Joel A.C. and Stephen J. Mezias. 1992. Localized competition and organizational failure in the Manhattan hotel industry, 1898–1990. *Administrative Science Quarterly* 37: 580–604.

Baum, Joel A.C., and Christine Oliver. 1991. Institutional linkages and organizational mortality. *Administrative Science Quarterly* 37: 580–604.

———. 1992. Institutional embeddedness and the dynamics of organizational populations. *American Sociological Review* 57: 540–559.

Baum, Joel A.C., and Jitendra V. Singh. 1994. Organization-environment coevolution. In *Evolutionary dynamics of organizations* edited by J.A.C. Baum and J.V. Singh, 379–402. New York: Oxford.

Belasco, W.J. 1979. *Americans on the road*. Cambridge, MA: The MIT Press.

Beniger, James R. 1986. *The control revolution*. Cambridge, MA: Harvard.

Boeker, Warren. 1991. Organizational strategy: An ecological perspective. *Academy of Management Journal* 34:613–635.

Brint, Steven, and Jerome Karabel. 1991. Institutional origins and transformations: The case of American community colleges. In *The new institutionalism in organizational analysis* edited by W.W. Powell and P.J. DiMaggio, 337–360. Chicago: University of Chicago Press.

Brüderl, Josef, and Rudolf Schüssler. 1990. Organizational mortality: The liabilities of newness and adolescence. *Administrative Science Quarterly* 35:530–547.

Cameron, Colin A., and Praveen K. Trivedi. 1986. Econometric models based on count data: Comparisons and applications of some estimators and tests. *Journal of Applied Econometrics* 1: 29–53.

———. 1990. Regression-based tests for overdispersion in the Poisson model. *Journal of Econometrics* 46: 347–364.

Caraux, Laurent P. 1976. Cash management in the hotel industry: A system approach for the chain organization. Masters thesis, School of Hotel Administration, Cornell University.

Carroll, Glenn R., and Jacques Delacroix. 1982. Organizational mortality in the newspaper industries of Ireland and Argentina. *Administrative Science Quarterly* 27:169–198.

Carroll, Glenn R., and Michael T. Hannan. 1989. Density dependence in the evolution of populations of newspaper organizations. *American Sociological Review* 54:524–541.

Chandler, Alfred D., Jr. 1977. *The visible hand.* Cambridge, MA: Belknap.

———. 1981. Historical determinants of managerial hierarchies: Response to Perrow. In *Perspectives on organizational design and behavior* edited by A.H. Van de Ven and W.F. Joyce, 391–402. New York: Wiley.

Clarenbach, Ernst. 1907. Clarenbach's system of hotel accounting. *Hotel Monthly* 15, no. 170 (May, 1907): 18–24.

Coase, Ronald H. 1937. The nature of the firm. *Econometrica* 16:386–405.

Coleman, James S. 1968. The mathematical study of change. In *Methodology in social research*, edited by H.M. Blalock, Jr. and A. Blalock, 428–478. New York: Mcgraw Hill.

———. 1990. *Foundations of Social Theory.* Cambridge, MA: Belknap Press.

Cornell University Archives. #28/1/1803. Ithaca, NY.

Cornell University. 1896–1980. *Registrar's report.* Ithaca, NY: Cornell University.

Daems, Herman. 1983. The determinants of the hierarchical organization of industry. In *Power, efficiency and institutions* edited by A. Francis and J. Turk, 35–53. London: Heinemann.

Daft, Richard L., and Selwyn Becker. 1978. School district size and the deployment of personnel resources. *The Alberta Journal of Educational Research* 24:173–187.

Davis, Lance E. and Douglass C. North. 1971. *Institutional change and American economic growth.* New York: Cambridge.

DiMaggio, Paul J. 1988. Interest and agency in institutional theory. In *Institutional patterns and organizations: Culture and environment* edited by L.G. Zucker, 3–21. Cambridge, MA: Ballinger.

———. 1991. Constructing an organizational field as a professional project: U.S. art museums, 1920–1940. In *The new institutionalism in organizational analysis* edited by W.W. Powell and P.J. DiMaggio, 267–292. Chicago: University of Chicago Press.

DiMaggio, Paul J., and Walter W. Powell. 1983. The iron cage revisited: Institutional isomorphism and collective rationality in organizational fields. *American Sociological Review* 48:146–160.

Emery, F.E., and E.L. Trist. 1965. The causal texture of organizational environments. *Human Relations* 18: 21–31.

Frank, Robert H. 1988. *Passions within reason*. New York: W.W. Norton

Freeman, John, Glenn R. Carroll, and Michael T. Hannan. 1983. The liability of newness: Age dependence in organizational death rates. *American Sociological Review* 48: 692–710.

Freeman, John, and Michael T. Hannan. 1975. Growth and decline processes in organizations. *American Sociological Review* 40:215–228.

———. 1983. Niche width and the dynamics of organizational populations. *American Journal of Sociology* 88: 1117–1145.

———. 1989. Setting the record straight on organizational ecology: Rebuttal to Young. *American Journal of Sociology* 95:425–435.

Geller, Neal A. 1991. *Internal control: A fraud prevention handbook for hotel and restaurant managers*. Ithaca, NY: Cornell School of Hotel Administration.

Gibbons, Robert. 1992. *Game theory for applied economists*. Princeton, NJ: Princeton University Press.

Gordon, Robert A., and James Edwin Howell. 1959. *Higher education for business*. New York: Columbia.

Granovetter, Mark. 1985. Economic action and social structure: The problem of embeddedness. *American Journal of Sociology* 91:481–510.

———. 1991. Economic institutions as social constructions: A framework for analyses. Paper presented at the CREA conference on The Economics of Conventions, 27–28 May, Paris.

Greene, William H. *Econometric Analysis*. New York: Macmillan.

———. 1992. *Limdep: Users manual and reference guide*. Bellport, NY: Econometric Software.

Hamilton, Gary G., and Nicole Woolsey Biggart. 1988. Market, culture and authority: A comparative analysis of management and organization in the Far East. *American Journal of Sociology* 94: S52–S94.

Hannan, Michael T. 1988. Age dependence in the mortality of national labor unions: Comparisons of parametric models. *Journal of Mathematical Sociology* 14:1–30.

Hannan, Michael T., and Glenn R. Carroll. 1992. *Dynamics of organizational populations: Density, competition and legitimation*. New York: Oxford University Press.

Hannan, Michael T. and John Freeman. 1977. The population ecology of organizations. *American Journal of Sociology* 82: 929–964.

———. 1984. Structural inertia and organizational change. *American Sociological Review* 49: 149–164.

———. 1987. The ecology of organizational founding: American labor unions, 1836–1985. *American Journal of Sociology* 92: 910–943.

———. 1988. The ecology of organizational mortality: American labor unions, 1836–1985. *American Journal of Sociology* 94:25–52.

———. 1989. *Organizational Ecology*. Cambridge, MA: Harvard Press.

Haveman, Heather A. 1993a. Follow the leader: Mimetic isomorphism and entry into new markets. *Administrative Science Quarterly* 38:593–627.

———. 1993b. Organizational size and change: Diversification in the savings and loan industry after deregulation. *Administrative Science Quarterly* 38:20–50.

Hawley, Amos. 1950. *Community ecology: A theory of community structure*. New York: Ronald Press.

Hayner, Norman S. 1936. *Hotel Life*. Chapel Hill, NC: University of North Carolina Press.

Holm, Petter. 1995. The dynamics of institutionalization: Transformation processes in Norwegian fisheries. *Administrative Science Quarterly* 40: 398–422.

Horwath and Horwath. 1968. *Hotel Operations*. New York: Horwath & Horwath.

Horwath, Ernest B., and Louis Toth. 1928. *Hotel Accounting*. New York: Ronald Press.

Horwath Hotel Accountant. 1930. The fifteenth anniversary of H & H. *Horwath Hotel Accountant* 10, no. 8:1–9.

Hotel Monthly. 1902. Saiter's duplicate room chart sheets. Hotel Monthly 10, no. 112 (July, 1902):27.

———. 1903. Stewards third annual. *Hotel Monthly* 11, no. 127 (October, 1903):28–29.

———. 1906. Letter to the editor. *Hotel Monthly* 14, no. 156 (March, 1906):43.

———. 1912. Warden system of controlling the bar. *Hotel Monthly* 20, no. 227 (February, 1912):66–67.

———. 1939. Why the 'Boss way' makes Boss hotels pay. *Hotel Monthly* 47, no. 553 (February, 1939):21–27.

Hotel Redbook. 1896–1927. *Hotel Redbook.* New York: Official Hotel Red Book and Directory Co.

———. 1928–1981. *Hotel Redbook.* New York: American Hotel Association Directory Corporation.

Ingram, Paul. 1993a. Institutional creation and change: A test of the rational actor explanation. Cornell University. Photocopy.

———. 1993b. Old, tired, and ready to die: The age dependence of organizational mortality reconsidered. Paper presented at the Academy of Management Annual Meetings, August, Atlanta Ga.

———. 1996. Internal control and the rise of hotel chains. Carnegie Mellon University. Photocopy.

———. 1997. Changing the rules: Interests, organizations and institutional change in the U.S. hospitality industry. In *The new institutionalism in economic sociology* edited by M. Brinton and V. Nee, forthcoming. New York: Russell Sage Foundation.

Ingram, Paul, and Crist Inman. 1997. Institutions, intergroup competition and the evolution of organizational populations. *Administrative Science Quarterly*, forthcoming.

Inman, Crist. 1993. Shifting patterns of social order: The creation of current rules and roles governing hospitality. Cornell University. Photocopy.

Jensen, Michael C., and William H. Meckling. 1976. Theory of the firm: Managerial behavior, agency costs and ownership structure. *Journal of Financial Economics* 3:305–360.

Kerley, N. 1949. *The Milner Story.* Detroit: Milner Hotels Management Co., Inc.

King, Gary. 1988. Statistical models for political science event counts: Bias in conventional procedures and evidence for the exponential poisson regression model. *American Journal of Political Science* 32:838–863.

Kmenta, Jan. 1986. *Elements of econometrics (2nd ed.).* New York: Macmillan.

Lebhar, Godfrey M. 1959. *Chain stores in America, 1859–1959.* New York: Chain Store Publishing Corporation.

Levinthal, Daniel. 1991. Random walks and organizational mortality. *Administrative Science Quarterly* 35:397–420.

Lewis, Sinclair. 1919. *Free Air*. New York: Grosset and Dunlap.

Meyer, John W., and Brian Rowan. 1977. Institutionalized organizations: Formal structure as myth and ceremony. *American Journal of Sociology* 83:340–363.

Meyer, John W., and W. Richard Scott. 1983. *Organizational environments: ritual and rationality*. Beverly Hills, CA: Sage.

Moon, Germaine L. Ramounachou. 1980. *Barstow depots and Harvey Houses*. Barstow, CA: Mohave River Valley Museum Association.

Nee, Victor, and Paul Ingram. 1997. Beyond embeddedness: Institutions, exchange and social structure. In *The new institutionalism in economic sociology* edited by M. Brinton and V. Nee, forthcoming. New York: Russell Sage Foundation.

North, Douglass C. 1990. *Institutions, institutional change and economic performance*. New York: Cambridge University Press.

Oliver, Christine. 1991. Strategic responses to institutional processes. *Academy of Management Review* 16:145–179.

Ostrom, Charles W. Jr. 1990. *Time series analysis: Regression techniques (2nd ed.)*. Newbury Park, CA: Sage.

Perrow, Charles. 1981. Markets, hierarchies and hegemony. In *Perspectives on organizational design and behavior* edited by A.H. Van de Ven and W.F. Joyce, 371–386. New York: Wiley.

———. 1986. *Complex organizations: A critical essay (3rd ed.)*. New York: Random House.

Pfeffer, Jeffrey, and Gerald R. Salancik. 1978. *The external control of organizations: A resource dependence perspective*. New York: Harper & Row.

Podd, George. 1950. Accounting: The new science in hotel keeping. *Southern Hotel Journal* (April):22–27.

Podolny, Joel M., and Toby E. Stuart. 1994. A role-based ecology of technological change. *American Journal of Sociology* 10:1224–1260.

Ranger-Moore, James. 1991. Bigger may be better but is older wiser? Age dependence in organizational death rates. Department of Sociology, University of Arizona. Photocopy.

Rohwer, Götz. 1993. *TDA (Transitional Data Analysis* 5.2. Florence: European University Institute.

Sayles, Charles I., and H. Alexander MacLennan. 1966. *A new hotel management system based upon data processing in a computer center*. School of Hotel Administration: Ithaca, NY.

Scharfstein, David S., and Jeremy C. Stein. 1990. Herd behavior and investment. *American Economic Review* 80:465–479.

Schmookler, Jacob. 1966. *Invention and economic growth*. Cambridge, MA: Harvard.

Scott, W. Richard. 1987a. The adolescence of institutional theory. *Administrative Science Quarterly* 32:493–511.

———. 1987b. *Organizations: Rational, natural, and open systems*. Englewood-Cliffs, NJ: Prentice-Hall.

Simon, Herbert A. 1957. *Models of Man*. New York: Wiley.

Singh, Jitendra V., Robert J. House, and David J. Tucker. 1986. Organizational change and organizational mortality. *Administrative Science Quarterly* 31:587–611.

Singh, Jitendra V., David J. Tucker, and Robert J. House. 1986. Organizational legitimacy and the liability of newness. *Administrative Science Quarterly* 31:17–93.

Stigler, George J. 1971. The theory of economic regulation. *Bell Journal of Economics and Management Science* 2:3–21.

Stinchcombe, Arthur L. 1965. Organizations and social structure. In *Handbook of Organizations* edited by In J.G. March, 142–193. Chicago: Rand McNally.

Strang, David. 1987. The administrative transformation of American education: School district consolidation, 1938–1980. *Administrative Science Quarterly* 32:352–366.

Surety Association of America. Archives in Iselin, NJ.

Terreberry, Shirley. 1968. The evolution of organizational environments. *Administrative Science Quarterly* 12:590–613.

Tolbert, Pamela. 1985. Institutional environments and resource dependence: Sources of administrative structure in institutions of higher education. *Administrative Science Quarterly* 30:1–13.

Tolbert, Pamela S., and Lynne G. Zucker. 1983. Institutional sources of change in the formal structure of organizations: The diffusion of civil service reform, 1880–1935. *Administrative Science Quarterly* 28:22–39.

Tuma, Nancy B., and Michael T. Hannan. 1984. *Social Dynamics*. New York: Academic Press.

Uhrbrock, Richard S. 1930. Personnel conscious' hotelmen have made much progress in scientific labor management. *Hotel Industry* July: 9–11.

U.S. Bureau of Census. 1933, 1935. *Census of American business*. Washington, D.C.: Government Printing Office.

———. 1940, 1948, 1954, 1958, 1963, 1967. *Census of business*. Washington, D.C.: Government Printing Office.

———. 1972. *Census of selected services*. Washington, D.C.: Government Printing Office.

———. 1977, 1982, 1987. *Census of service industries*. Washington, D.C.: Government Printing Office.

Van de Ven, Andrew H. and Raghu Garud. 1993. Innovation and industry development: The case of Cochlear Implants. Working Paper, Strategic Management Research Center, University of Minnesota.

Western Hotel Reporter. 1910. Our New York Letter, *Western Hotel Reporter* 9, no. 2 (July 9, 1919):5.

Whetten, David A. 1987. Organizational growth and decline processes. *Annual Review of Sociology* 12: 335–358.

Williamson, Oliver E. 1975. *Markets and hierarchies*. New York: Free Press.

———. 1979. Transaction-cost economics: The governance of contractual relations. *Journal of Law and Economics* 12:233–262.

Williamson, Oliver E. and William G. Ouchi. 1981a. The markets and hierarchies and visible hand perspectives. In Perspectives on organizational design and behavior edited by A.H. Van de Ven and W.F. Joyce, 347–370. New York: Wiley.

———. 1981b. Rejoinder to Perrow. In Perspectives on organizational design and behavior edited by A.H. Van de Ven and W.F. Joyce, 387–390. New York: Wiley.

Willy, John. 1903. Editorial. *Hotel Monthly* 9, no. 124 (July, 1903):18.

———. 1905. Editorial. Hotel Monthly 13, no.149 (August, 1905):18.

Young, Ruth C. 1988. Is population ecology a useful paradigm for the study of organizations? *American Journal of Sociology* 94:1–25.

Young and Rubicam, Inc. 1948. *Roadside housing survey*. New York: American Hotel Association.

Zald, Mayer N. 1970. Political economy: A framework for comparative analysis. In *Power in Organizations* edited by M.N. Zald. Nashville, TN: Vanderbilt University Press.

Zucker, Lynne G. 1989. Combining institutional theory and population ecology: No legitimacy, no history. *American Sociological Review* 54: 542–545.

Index